Proposed Amendments to the U.S. Constitution 1787-2021

IN FOUR VOLUMES

Supplement Volume IV
2001-2021

Proposed Amendments to the U.S. Constitution 1787-2021

John R. Vile, Editor

IN FOUR VOLUMES

Supplement Volume IV 2001-2021

THE LAWBOOK EXCHANGE, LTD.
Clark, New Jersey

ISBN 978-1-58477-225-5 (Set)
ISBN 978-1-61619-141-2 (Vol.I)
ISBN 978-1-61619-142-9 (Vol.II)
ISBN 978-1-61619-143-6 (Vol.III)
ISBN 978-1-61619-657-8 (Vol.IV Supplement)

Lawbook Exchange edition 2021

THE LAWBOOK EXCHANGE, LTD.
33 Terminal Avenue
Clark, New Jersey 07066-1321

Please see our website for a selection of our other publications and fine facsimile reprints of classic works of legal history:
www.lawbookexchange.com

Library of Congress Cataloging-in-Publication Data

Proposed amendments to the U.S. Constitution: 1787-2001 / John R. Vile, editor.
p. cm.
Includes bibliographical references and index.
ISBN 1-58477-225-5 (cloth: alk. paper)
1. Constitutional amendments—United States. I. Title: Proposed amendments to the US
Constitution. II. Title: Proposed amendments to the United States Constitution.
III. Vile, John R.

KF4557 .P76 2002
342.73'035—dc21 2002040563

Printed in the United States of America on acid-free paper

General Contents

Volume I

Volume II

Volume III

Supplement Volume IV

Proposed Amendments to the United States Constitution, second half of 107th- 112th Congresses (2001-2021)

Contents

Volume IV (Supplement 2001-2021)

[Replaces previous supplement 2001—2010]

Introduction

This work updates a supplement published in 2011, to the three-volume set of *Proposed Amendments to the U.S. Constitution, 1787-2001*, which the Law Book Exchange first published in 2003 and which it republished in 2011 with a more colorful cover and my original supplement. The original supplement covered the years from 2001 to 2010. This new supplement, which is designed as a replacement, represents a continuing effort to track amendments that members of Congress have proposed throughout the history of the republic by supplementing the proposed amendments from 2001 to 2010 with those that have been introduced in Congress through mid-2021.

The information in this supplement makes no pretense to originality. I have taken most of this material directly from the Congress.Govs website. Because constitutional amendments require proposal by two-thirds majorities in both houses of Congress, prior to being sent to the states three fourths of which must ratify before the amendments become law, members of Congress introduce most of these in the form of Joint Resolutions. Since these are not the only subject of such resolutions, I have weeded out those resolutions that did not deal with amendments. Thus, there are often gaps between the numbers of the H.J. and S.J numbers in this volume.

As with the earlier supplement, which in incorporated into this one, I have otherwise left the materials in the form that I found them except for two particulars. First, I deleted references to the committee to which each resolution was referred (almost invariably either the House or Senate Judiciary Committee) as well as most subsequent actions taken by that body. Second, I have added both a subject and a sponsor index to the proposals in this volume to facilitate further research.

The original three volumes tracked the number of amending proposals that members of Congress have introduced. Because the last volume of that work was published in the middle of the 107th Congress (2001-2002), this volume continues the numbering system used there, the last component of which began with the 102nd Congress (1991-1992), and thus now roughly covers a 30-year period. The last compilation in the third volume ended on number 691, so this, like the supplement it replaces, begins with 692. This number does not correspond to a number on the Library of Congress website but is added purely for indexing purposes. The proposals that have been added since the last supplement begin with 1002.

I have only listed each proposal once even though many of them have several parts and cover more than a single subject. Thus a proposal to limit congressional terms may be combined with one to extend a single term of a member of the House of Representatives from two years to four years; it may limit the total number of terms or the total number of consecutive terms. A proposal for better housing might also refer to health care or education. Similarly, there is wide variation among the mechanisms that members of Congress have proposed to achieve a balanced budget, increase voting access, or regulate campaign contributions and expenditures. Individuals interested in researching any of these topics in depth will need to be alert to related proposals.

As readers will see, the most popular proposed amendments (at least judging by the number of times they have been introduced) continue to those dealing with balanced budgets, with campaign financing and reform, and (ironic as it may seem) with congressional term limits. There have been increasing calls to waive the original ratification deadline for the Equal Rights Amendment. I have designated these proposals with an asterisk, to indicate that they vary somewhat from proposing a new amendment.

As a perusal of the sponsors will show, many propose the same amendment session after session, some rarely propose constitutional amendments, and some do so on a regular basis. Since the last publication of this supplement, the nation has gone another ten years without proposing or ratifying any constitutional amendments by the requisite majorities, although it has been roiled by a very unconventional president who was twice impeached during his single term in office, an attack by a mob on the U.S. Capitol contesting his electoral defeat, and continuing efforts at the state level to restrict voting rights.

Although this volume focuses on the number of proposals that members of Congress have introduced, it is important to recognize that the prestige and position within Congress of the individual introducing an amendment and its number of co-sponsors might be far more important than the number of times that members of Congress have introduced it. Moreover, it is always possible that members of Congress are introducing amendments more for their symbolic value than in any real hope that they will be adopted. Still, a perusal of amending proposals provides a window both on issues that persist over time and those that arise out of particular controversies.

Americans are blessed to live in a nation that provides both a system of regularized elections and a legal mechanisms for constitutional change. At the Constitutional Convention of 1787, after the Federalist-Anti-Federalist debates, after the Civil War, during the Progressive Era, and at other times in U.S. history, Americans have adopted a new Constitution or constitutional amendments to promote a more perfect Union. At each of these times, and others, they have had to decide what parts of the system to preserve and which ones to change. Although the Founders have been criticized for making the amending process too difficult, their goal was that of striking a balance between precipitate change for the sake of change and a system that was too rigid. As the gap between the Seneca Falls Convention for women's rights in 1848 and the ratification of the Nineteenth Amendment in 1920 demonstrates, constitutional amendments sometimes take a long time to percolate. To mix metaphors, the proposals in this supplement and the previous volumes are a virtual seedbed of possibilities that make their study not simply one of academic interest but also one of potential political consequence.

John R. Vile,
Middle Tennessee State University

107th Congress (2001-2002)

Beginning from end of last volume

House

692. H.J.RES.72
Proposing an amendment to the Constitution of the United States regarding the right to vote.
Sponsor: Rep Jackson, Jesse L., Jr. [D, IL-2] (introduced 1/6/2001)
Cosponsors (None)

693. H.J.RES.77
Proposing an amendment to the Constitution of the United States regarding the appointment of individuals to serve as Members of the House of Representatives when, in a national emergency, a significant number of Members are unable to serve.
Sponsor: Rep Lofgren, Zoe [D, CA-16] (introduced 12/5/2001)
Cosponsors (None)

694. H.J.RES.81
Proposing an amendment to the Constitution of the United States restoring religious freedom.
Sponsor: Rep Istook, Ernest J., Jr. [R, OK-5] (introduced 12/20/2001)
Cosponsors (88)

695. H.J.RES.85
Proposing an amendment to the Constitution to provide for a balanced budget for the United States Government and for greater accountability in the enactment of tax legislation.
Sponsor: Rep Berry, Marion [D, AR-1] (introduced 3/12/2002)
Cosponsors (17)

696. H.J.RES.86
Proposing a balanced budget amendment to the Constitution of the United States.
Sponsor: Rep Istook, Ernest J., Jr. [R, OK-5] (introduced 4/11/2002)
Cosponsors (127)

697. H.J.RES.88
Proposing an amendment to the Constitution of the United States to protect the rights of crime victims.
Sponsor: Rep Royce, Edward R. [R, CA-39] (introduced 4/23/2002)
Cosponsors (None)

698. H.J.RES.90
Proposing an amendment to the Constitution to provide for a balanced budget for the United States Government and for greater accountability in the enactment of tax legislation.
Sponsor: Rep Berry, Marion [D, AR-1] (introduced 4/25/2002)
Cosponsors (20)

699. H.J.RES.91
Proposing an amendment to the Constitution of the United States to protect the rights of crime victims.
Sponsor: Rep Chabot, Steve [R, OH-1] (introduced 5/2/2002)
Cosponsors (22)

700. H.J.RES.93
Proposing an amendment to the Constitution of the United States relating to marriage.
Sponsor: Rep Shows, Ronnie [D, MS-4] (introduced 5/15/2002)
Cosponsors (22)

701. H.J.RES.96
Proposing a tax limitation amendment to the Constitution of the United States.
Sponsor: Rep Sessions, Pete [R, TX-5] (introduced 6/6/2002)
Cosponsors (155)

702. H.J.RES.99
Proposing a spending limitation amendment to the Constitution of the United States.
Sponsor: Rep Smith, Nick [R, MI-7] (introduced 6/18/2002)
Cosponsors (None)

703. H.J.RES.102
Proposing an amendment to the Constitution of the United States to guarantee the right to recite the Pledge of Allegiance to the Flag.
Sponsor: Rep Pickering, Charles W. "Chip" [R, MS-3] (introduced

6/26/2002)

Cosponsors (13)

704. H.J.RES.103
Proposing an amendment to the Constitution of the United States with respect to the Pledge of Allegiance.
Sponsor: Rep Green, Gene [D, TX-29] (introduced 6/27/2002)

Cosponsors (None)

705. H.J.RES.104
Proposing an amendment to the Constitution of the United States to protect the Pledge of Allegiance.
Sponsor: Rep Lucas, Frank D. [R, OK-6] (introduced 6/27/2002)

Cosponsors (1)

706. H.J.RES.106
Proposing an amendment to the Constitution of the United States respecting real and virtual child pornography.
Sponsor: Rep Brown, Henry E., Jr. [R, SC-1] (introduced 7/17/2002)

Cosponsors (37)

707. H.J.RES.108
Proposing an amendment to the Constitution of the United States to guarantee the right to use and recite the Pledge of Allegiance to the Flag and the national motto.
Sponsor: Rep Pickering, Charles W. "Chip" [R, MS-3] (introduced 7/25/2002)

Cosponsors (25)

Senate

708. S.J.RES.33

A joint resolution proposing an amendment to the Constitution of the United States relating to contributions and expenditures intended to affect elections.

Sponsor: Sen Hollings, Ernest F. [D, SC] (introduced 3/4/2002)

Cosponsors (9)

709. S.J.RES.35

A joint resolution proposing an amendment to the Constitution of the United States to protect the rights of crime victims.

Sponsor: Sen Feinstein, Dianne [D, CA] (introduced 4/15/2002)

Cosponsors (28)

710. S.J.RES.39

A joint resolution proposing an amendment to the Constitution of the United States relative to the reference to God in the Pledge of Allegiance and on United States currency.

Sponsor: Sen Landrieu, Mary L. [D, LA] (introduced 6/26/2002)

Cosponsors (1)

711. S.J.RES.43

A joint resolution proposing an amendment to the Constitution of the United States to guarantee the right to use and recite the Pledge of Allegiance to the Flag and the national motto.

Sponsor: Sen Lott, Trent [R, MS] (introduced 8/1/2002)

Cosponsors (None)

108th Congress (2003-2004)

House

712. H.J.RES.4
Proposing an amendment to the Constitution of the United States authorizing the Congress to prohibit the physical desecration of the flag of the United States.
Sponsor: Rep Cunningham, Randy (Duke) [R, CA-50] (introduced 1/7/2003)
Cosponsors (213)

713. H.J.RES.5
Proposing an amendment to the Constitution of the United States to permit the Congress to limit expenditures in elections for Federal office.
Sponsor: Rep Dingell, John D. [D, MI-15] (introduced 1/7/2003)
Cosponsors (None)

714. H.J.RES.6
Proposing an amendment to the Constitution to provide for a balanced budget for the United States Government and for greater accountability in the enactment of tax legislation.
Sponsor: Rep Emerson, Jo Ann [R, MO-8] (introduced 1/7/2003)
Cosponsors (1)

715. H.J.RES.7
Proposing an amendment to the Constitution of the United States relating to voluntary school prayer.
Sponsor: Rep Emerson, Jo Ann [R, MO-8] (introduced 1/7/2003)
Cosponsors (1)

716. H.J.RES.8
Proposing an amendment to the Constitution of the United States authorizing the Congress and the States to prohibit the act of desecration of the flag of the United States and to set criminal penalties for that act.
Sponsor: Rep Emerson, Jo Ann [R, MO-8] (introduced 1/7/2003)
Cosponsors (2)

717. H.J.RES.9
Proposing an amendment to the Constitution of the United States with respect to the right to life.
Sponsor: Rep Emerson, Jo Ann [R, MO-8] (introduced 1/7/2003)
Cosponsors (3)

718. H.J.RES.10
Proposing an amendment to the Constitution of the United States to protect the rights of crime victims.
Sponsor: Rep Royce, Edward R. [R, CA-40] (introduced 1/7/2003)
Cosponsors (2)

719. H.J.RES.11
Proposing an amendment to the Constitution of the United States to repeal the twenty-second article of amendment, thereby removing the limitation on the number of terms an individual may serve as President.
Sponsor: Rep Serrano, Jose E. [D, NY-16] (introduced 1/7/2003)
Cosponsors (3)

720. H.J.RES.14
Proposing an amendment to the Constitution of the United States to provide that Federal judges be reconfirmed by the Senate every 10 years.
Sponsor: Rep Hefley, Joel [R, CO-5] (introduced 1/27/2003)
Cosponsors (None)

721. H.J.RES.15
Proposing an amendment to the Constitution of the United States relative to abolishing personal income, estate, and gift taxes and prohibiting the United States Government from engaging in business in competition with its citizens.
Sponsor: Rep Paul, Ron [R, TX-14] (introduced 1/28/2003)
Cosponsors (2)

722. H.J.RES.16
Proposing an amendment to the Constitution of the United States to limit the number of consecutive terms that a Member of Congress may serve.
Sponsor: Rep Platts, Todd Russell [R, PA-19] (introduced 1/29/2003)
Cosponsors (None)

723. H.J.RES.21
Proposing an amendment to the Constitution of the United States regarding regulations on the amounts of expenditures of personal funds made by candidates for election for public office.
Sponsor: Rep Leach, James A. [R, IA-2] (introduced 2/5/2003)
Cosponsors (None)

724. H.J.RES.22
Proposing a balanced budget amendment to the Constitution of the United States.
Sponsor: Rep Istook, Ernest J., Jr. [R, OK-5] (introduced 2/13/2003)
Cosponsors (133)

725. H.J.RES.25
Proposing an amendment to the Constitution of the United States to repeal the 22nd amendment to the Constitution.
Sponsor: Rep Hoyer, Steny H. [D, MD-5] (introduced 2/25/2003)
Cosponsors (7)

726. H.J.RES.26
Proposing an amendment to the Constitution of the United States to protect the Pledge of Allegiance.
Sponsor: Rep Lucas, Frank D. [R, OK-3] (introduced 2/27/2003)
Cosponsors (2)

727. H.J.RES.28
Proposing an amendment to the Constitution of the United States regarding the right to vote.
Sponsor: Rep Jackson, Jesse L., Jr. [D, IL-2] (introduced 3/4/2003)
Cosponsors (45)

728. H.J.RES.29
Proposing an amendment to the Constitution of the United States regarding the right of all citizens of the United States to a public education of equal high quality.
Sponsor: Rep Jackson, Jesse L., Jr. [D, IL-2] (introduced 3/4/2003)
Cosponsors (37)

729. H.J.RES.30
Proposing an amendment to the Constitution of the United States regarding the right of citizens of the United States to health care of equal

high quality.
Sponsor: Rep Jackson, Jesse L., Jr. [D, IL-2] (introduced 3/4/2003)
Cosponsors (35)

730. H.J.RES.31

Proposing an amendment to the Constitution of the United States relating to equality of rights and reproductive rights.
Sponsor: Rep Jackson, Jesse L., Jr. [D, IL-2] (introduced 3/4/2003)
Cosponsors (5)

731. H.J.RES.32

Proposing an amendment to the Constitution of the United States respecting the right to decent, safe, sanitary, and affordable housing.
Sponsor: Rep Jackson, Jesse L., Jr. [D, IL-2] (introduced 3/4/2003)
Cosponsors (5)

732. H.J.RES.33

Proposing an amendment to the Constitution of the United States respecting the right to a clean, safe, and sustainable environment.
Sponsor: Rep Jackson, Jesse L., Jr. [D, IL-2] (introduced 3/4/2003)
Cosponsors (5)

733. H.J.RES.34

Proposing an amendment to the Constitution of the United States relative to taxing the people of the United States progressively.
Sponsor: Rep Jackson, Jesse L., Jr. [D, IL-2] (introduced 3/4/2003)
Cosponsors (5)

734. H.J.RES.35

Proposing an amendment to the Constitution of the United States respecting the right to full employment and balanced growth.
Sponsor: Rep Jackson, Jesse L., Jr. [D, IL-2] (introduced 3/4/2003)
Cosponsors (5)

735. H.J.RES.37

Proposing an amendment to the Constitution of the United States relative to equal rights for men and women.
Sponsor: Rep Maloney, Carolyn B. [D, NY-14] (introduced 3/12/2003)
Cosponsors (202)

736. H.J.RES.39

Proposing an amendment to the Constitution of the United States relative to references to God in the Pledge of Allegiance and on United States coins and currency.

Sponsor: Rep Carter, John R. [R, TX-31] (introduced 3/13/2003)

Cosponsors (None)

737. H.J.RES.40

Proposing an amendment to the Constitution of the United States to guarantee the right to use and recite the Pledge of Allegiance to the Flag and the national motto.

Sponsor: Rep Pickering, Charles W. "Chip" [R, MS-3] (introduced 3/18/2003)

Cosponsors (11)

738. H.J.RES.42

Proposing an amendment to the Constitution of the United States to deny United States citizenship to individuals born in the United States to parents who are neither United States citizens nor persons who owe permanent allegiance to the United States.

Sponsor: Rep Paul, Ron [R, TX-14] (introduced 3/20/2003)

Cosponsors (4)

739. H.J.RES.43

Proposing an amendment to the Constitution of the United States to limit the number of terms that a Member of Congress may serve.

Sponsor: Rep Vitter, David [R, LA-1] (introduced 3/26/2003)

Cosponsors (None)

740. H.J.RES.44

Proposing an amendment to the Constitution of the United States to provide that no person born in the United States will be a United States citizen unless a parent is a United States citizen, or is lawfully admitted for permanent residence in the United States, at the time of the birth.

Sponsor: Rep Foley, Mark [R, FL-16] (introduced 3/31/2003)

Cosponsors (16)

741. H.J.RES.46

Proposing an amendment to the Constitution of the United States restoring religious freedom.

Sponsor: Rep Istook, Ernest J., Jr. [R, OK-5] (introduced 4/9/2003)

Cosponsors (103)

742. H.J.RES.47
Proposing an amendment to the Constitution of the United States respecting the right to a home.
Sponsor: Rep Rangel, Charles B. [D, NY-15] (introduced 4/9/2003)
Cosponsors (None)

743. H.J.RES.48
Proposing an amendment to the Constitution of the United States to protect the rights of crime victims.
Sponsor: Rep Chabot, Steve [R, OH-1] (introduced 4/10/2003)
Cosponsors (23)

744. H.J.RES.50
Proposing a tax limitation amendment to the Constitution of the United States.
Sponsor: Rep Sessions, Pete [R, TX-32] (introduced 4/10/2003)
Cosponsors (75)

745. H.J.RES.53
Proposing an amendment to the Constitution of the United States to require Members of Congress and the President to forfeit the compensation paid to them starting at the conclusion of each fiscal year until all of the general appropriations bills for the following fiscal year are enacted.
Sponsor: Rep Ose, Doug [R, CA-3] (introduced 4/12/2003)
Cosponsors (None)

746. H.J.RES.54
Proposing a tax limitation amendment to the Constitution of the United States.
Sponsor: Rep Ose, Doug [R, CA-3] (introduced 4/12/2003)
Cosponsors (None)

747. H.J.RES.55
Proposing an amendment to the Constitution of the United States to require that Federal district court judges be reconfirmed every ten years by the executive and legislative authorities of the State in which they serve.
Sponsor: Rep Culberson, John Abney [R, TX-7] (introduced 5/7/2003)
Cosponsors (None)

748. H.J.RES.56
Proposing an amendment to the Constitution of the United States relat-

ing to marriage.
Sponsor: Rep Musgrave, Marilyn N. [R, CO-4] (introduced 5/21/2003)
Cosponsors (131)

749. H.J.RES.59
Proposing an amendment to the Constitution of the United States to permit persons who are not natural-born citizens of the United States, but who have been citizens of the United States for at least 35 years, to be eligible to hold the offices of President and Vice President.
Sponsor: Rep Snyder, Vic [D, AR-2] (introduced 6/11/2003)
Cosponsors (6)

750. H.J.RES.60
Proposing an amendment to the Constitution of the United States to authorize the line item veto.
Sponsor: Rep Andrews, Robert E. [D, NJ-1] (introduced 6/16/2003)
Cosponsors (7)

751. H.J.RES.61
Proposing an amendment to the Constitution of the United States to abolish the Federal income tax.
Sponsor: Rep Johnson, Sam [R, TX-3] (introduced 6/24/2003)
Cosponsors (5)

752. H.J.RES.65
Proposing an amendment to the Constitution of the United States respecting real and virtual child pornography.
Sponsor: Rep Brown, Henry E., Jr. [R, SC-1] (introduced 7/18/2003)
Cosponsors (17)

753. H.J.RES.66
Proposing an amendment to the Constitution of the United States to provide for terms of office for Members of the House of Representatives.
Sponsor: Rep Stenholm, Charles W. [D, TX-17] (introduced 7/24/2003)
Cosponsors (2)

754. H.J.RES.67
Proposing an amendment to the Constitution of the United States to permit persons who are not natural-born citizens of the United States, but who have been citizens of the United States for at least 20 years, to

be eligible to hold the Office of President.
Sponsor: Rep Conyers, John, Jr. [D, MI-14] (introduced 9/3/2003)
Cosponsors (1)

755. H.J.RES.68
Proposing an amendment to the Constitution of the United States relating to school prayer.
Sponsor: Rep Murtha, John P. [D, PA-12] (introduced 9/17/2003)
Cosponsors (None)

756. H.J.RES.71
Proposing an amendment to the Constitution of the United States deeming Presidential nominees to be appointed at the time of nomination subject to disapproval by the Senate within 120 days of receiving the nomination from the President.
Sponsor: Rep McCotter, Thaddeus G. [R, MI-11] (introduced 10/1/2003)
Cosponsors (9)

757. H.J.RES.77
Proposing an amendment to the Constitution of the United States regarding the appointment of individuals to fill vacancies in the House of Representatives.
Sponsor: Rep Baird, Brian [D, WA-3] (introduced 11/19/2003)
Cosponsors (None)

758. H.J.RES.81
Proposing an amendment to the Constitution of the United States limiting the number of consecutive terms that a Senator or Representative may serve and providing for 4-year terms for Representatives.
Sponsor: Rep Owens, Major R. [D, NY-11] (introduced 11/21/2003)
Cosponsors (None)

759. H.J.RES.83
Proposing an amendment to the Constitution of the United States regarding the appointment of individuals to fill vacancies in the House of Representatives.
Sponsor: Rep Baird, Brian [D, WA-3] (introduced 12/8/2003)
Cosponsors (2)

760. H.J.RES.85
Proposing an amendment to the Constitution of the United States re-

lating to the maintenance of a system of social insurance that provides Social Security for its citizens.
Sponsor: Rep Michaud, Michael H. [D, ME-2] (introduced 1/20/2004)
Cosponsors (None)

761. H.J.RES.86
Proposing a balanced budget amendment to the Constitution of the United States.
Sponsor: Rep Jenkins, William L. [R, TN-1] (introduced 1/21/2004)
Cosponsors (None)

762. H.J.RES.88
Proposing an amendment to the Constitution of the United States to provide that certain trust funds are outside the budget of the United States.
Sponsor: Rep Taylor, Gene [D, MS-4] (introduced 1/28/2004)
Cosponsors (7)

763. H.J.RES.89
Proposing an amendment to the Constitution of the United States regarding the appointment of individuals to fill vacancies in the House of Representatives.
Sponsor: Rep Larson, John B. [D, CT-1] (introduced 3/11/2004)
Cosponsors (None)

764. H.J.RES.90
Proposing an amendment to the Constitution of the United States regarding the appointment of individuals to serve as Members of the House of Representatives when, in a national emergency, a significant number of Members are unable to serve.
Sponsor: Rep Lofgren, Zoe [D, CA-16] (introduced 3/11/2004)
Cosponsors (None)

765. H.J.RES.92
Proposing an amendment to the Constitution of the United States relating to Congressional succession.
Sponsor: Rep Rohrabacher, Dana [R, CA-46] (introduced 4/2/2004)
Cosponsors (None)

766. H.J.RES.94
Proposing an amendment to the Constitution of the United States to

establish English as the official language of the United States.
Sponsor: Rep Goode, Virgil H., Jr. [R, VA-5] (introduced 4/29/2004)
Cosponsors (12)

767. H.J.RES.96
Proposing an amendment to the Constitution of the United States regarding the appointment of individuals to serve as Members of the House of Representatives when, in a national emergency, a significant number of Members are unable to serve due to death, resignation, or incapacity.
Sponsor: Rep Lofgren, Zoe [D, CA-16] (introduced 5/4/2004)
Cosponsors (None)

768. H.J.RES.101
Proposing an amendment to the Constitution of the United States regarding presidential election voting rights for residents of all United States territories and commonwealths.
Sponsor: Rep Christensen, Donna M. [D, VI] (introduced 7/22/2004)
Cosponsors (2)

769. H.J.RES.103
Every Vote Counts Amendment
Sponsor: Rep Green, Gene [D, TX-29] (introduced 9/14/2004)
Cosponsors (9)

770. H.J.RES.104
Proposing an amendment to the Constitution of the United States to make eligible for the Office of President a person who is not a natural born citizen of the United States but has been a United States citizen for at least 20 years.
Sponsor: Rep Rohrabacher, Dana [R, CA-46] (introduced 9/15/2004)
Cosponsors (None)

771. H.J.RES.105
Proposing an amendment to the Constitution of the United States to lower the age qualification for Senators from 30 years of age to 21 years of age and for Members of the House of Representatives from 25 years of age to 21 years of age.
Sponsor: Rep English, Phil [R, PA-3] (introduced 9/15/2004)
Cosponsors (None)

772. H.J.RES.106

Proposing an amendment to the Constitution of the United States relating to marriage.

Sponsor: Rep Musgrave, Marilyn N. [R, CO-4] (introduced 9/23/2004)
Cosponsors (121)

773. H.J.RES.109

Proposing an amendment to the Constitution of the United States to provide for the direct election of the President and Vice President by the popular vote of all citizens of the United States regardless of place of residence.

Sponsor: Rep Jackson, Jesse L., Jr. [D, IL-2] (introduced 10/8/2004)
Cosponsors (6)

774. H.J.RES.112

Proposing an amendment to the Constitution of the United States to abolish the Electoral College and to provide for the direct election of the President and Vice President of the United States.

Sponsor: Rep Lofgren, Zoe [D, CA-16] (introduced 11/18/2004)
Cosponsors (None)

775. H.J.RES.113

Proposing an amendment to the Constitution of the United States relating to the process by which the House of Representatives chooses the President of the United States in the event no candidate receives a majority of the electoral votes.

Sponsor: Rep Sherman, Brad [D, CA-27] (introduced 11/18/2004)
Cosponsors (None)

Senate

776. S.J.RES.1
A joint resolution proposing an amendment to the Constitution of the United States to protect the rights of crime victims.
Sponsor: Sen Kyl, Jon [R, AZ] (introduced 1/7/2003)
Cosponsors (26)

777. S.J.RES.2
A joint resolution proposing an amendment to the Constitution of the United States to require a balanced budget and protect Social Security surpluses.
Sponsor: Sen Craig, Larry E. [R, ID] (introduced 1/7/2003)
Cosponsors (1)

778. S.J.RES.4
A joint resolution proposing an amendment to the Constitution of the United States authorizing Congress to prohibit the physical desecration of the flag of the United States.
Sponsor: Sen Hatch, Orrin G. [R, UT] (introduced 1/16/2003)
Cosponsors (56)

779. S.J.RES.5
A joint resolution proposing an amendment to the Constitution of the United States relating to contributions and expenditures intended to affect elections.
Sponsor: Sen Hollings, Ernest F. [D, SC] (introduced 1/23/2003)
Cosponsors (1)

780. S.J.RES.7
A joint resolution proposing an amendment to the Constitution of the United States relative to the reference to God in the Pledge of Allegiance and on United States currency.
Sponsor: Sen Landrieu, Mary L. [D, LA] (introduced 3/3/2003)
Cosponsors (3)

781. S.J.RES.11
A joint resolution proposing an amendment to the Constitution of the United States relative to equal rights for women and men.
Sponsor: Sen Kennedy, Edward M. [D, MA] (introduced 3/18/2003)
Cosponsors (21)

782. S.J.RES.15
A joint resolution proposing an amendment to the Constitution of the United States to make eligible for the Office of President a person who has been a United States citizen for 20 years.
Sponsor: Sen Hatch, Orrin G. [R, UT] (introduced 7/10/2003)
Cosponsors (None)

783. S.J.RES.23
A joint resolution proposing an amendment to the Constitution of the United States providing for the event that one-fourth of the members of either the House of Representatives or the Senate are killed or incapacitated.
Sponsor: Sen Cornyn, John [R, TX] (introduced 11/5/2003)
Cosponsors (1)

784. S.J.RES.25
A joint resolution proposing an amendment to the Constitution of the United States relative to the line item veto.
Sponsor: Sen Dole, Elizabeth [R, NC] (introduced 11/19/2003)
Cosponsors (None)

785. S.J.RES.26
A joint resolution proposing an amendment to the Constitution of the United States relating to marriage.
Sponsor: Sen Allard, Wayne [R, CO] (introduced 11/25/2003)
Cosponsors (10)

786. S.J.RES.29
A joint resolution proposing an amendment to the Constitution of the United States which requires (except during time of war and subject to suspension by the Congress) that the total amount of money expended by the United States during any fiscal year not exceed the amount of certain revenue received by the United States during such fiscal year and not exceed 20 per centum of the gross national product of the United States during the previous calendar year.
Sponsor: Sen Shelby, Richard C. [R, AL] (introduced 3/11/2004)
Cosponsors (None)

787. S.J.RES.30
Marriage resolution [Federal Marriage Amendment: one man and one woman.]

Sponsor: Sen Allard, Wayne [R, CO] (introduced 3/22/2004)

Cosponsors (16)

788. S.J.RES.35

A joint resolution to repeal the seventeenth article of amendment to the Constitution of the United States.

Sponsor: Sen Miller, Zell [D, GA] (introduced 4/28/2004)

Cosponsors (None)

789. S.J.RES.40

Federal Marriage Amendment

Sponsor: Sen Allard, Wayne [R, CO] (introduced 7/7/2004)

Cosponsors (19)

109th Congress (2005-2006)

House

790. H.J.RES.1

Proposing an amendment to the Constitution of the United States regarding presidential election voting rights for residents of all United States territories and commonwealths.

Sponsor: Rep Christensen, Donna M. [D, VI] (introduced 1/4/2005)

Cosponsors (1)

791. H.J.RES.2

Proposing an amendment to the Constitution of the United States to permit persons who are not natural-born citizens of the United States, but who have been citizens of the United States for at least 20 years, to be eligible to hold the Office of President.

Sponsor: Rep Conyers, John, Jr. [D, MI-14] (introduced 1/4/2005)

Cosponsors (1)

792. H.J.RES.4

Proposing an amendment to the Constitution of the United States with respect to the right to life.

Sponsor: Rep Emerson, Jo Ann [R, MO-8] (introduced 1/4/2005)

Cosponsors (None)

793. H.J.RES.5

Proposing an amendment to the Constitution of the United States authorizing the Congress and the States to prohibit the act of desecration of the flag of the United States and to set criminal penalties for that act.

Sponsor: Rep Emerson, Jo Ann [R, MO-8] (introduced 1/4/2005)

Cosponsors (1)

794. H.J.RES.6

Proposing an amendment to the Constitution to provide for a balanced budget for the United States Government and for greater accountability in the enactment of tax legislation.

Sponsor: Rep Emerson, Jo Ann [R, MO-8] (introduced 1/4/2005)

Cosponsors (2)

795. H.J.RES.7
Proposing an amendment to the Constitution of the United States relating to voluntary school prayer.
Sponsor: Rep Emerson, Jo Ann [R, MO-8] (introduced 1/4/2005)
Cosponsors (1)

796. H.J.RES.8
Every Vote Counts Amendment
Sponsor: Rep Green, Gene [D, TX-29] (introduced 1/4/2005)
Cosponsors (2)

797. H.J.RES.9
Proposing an amendment to the Constitution of the United States to repeal the twenty-second article of amendment, thereby removing the limitation on the number of terms an individual may serve as President.
Sponsor: Rep Serrano, Jose E. [D, NY-16] (introduced 1/4/2005)
Cosponsors (None)

798. H.J.RES.10
Proposing an amendment to the Constitution of the United States authorizing the Congress to prohibit the physical desecration of the flag of the United States.
Sponsor: Rep Cunningham, Randy (Duke) [R, CA-50] (introduced 1/25/2005)
Cosponsors (196)

799. H.J.RES.11
Proposing an amendment to the Constitution of the United States to limit the number of consecutive terms that a Member of Congress may serve.
Sponsor: Rep Platts, Todd Russell [R, PA-19] (introduced 1/25/2005)
Cosponsors (None)

800. H.J.RES.13
Proposing an amendment to the Constitution of the United States regarding regulations on the amounts of expenditures of personal funds made by candidates for election for public office.
Sponsor: Rep Leach, James A. [R, IA-2] (introduced 1/26/2005)
Cosponsors (None)

801. H.J.RES.14
Proposing an amendment to the Constitution of the United States rela-

tive to abolishing personal income, estate, and gift taxes and prohibiting the United States Government from engaging in business in competition with its citizens.
Sponsor: Rep Paul, Ron [R, TX-14] (introduced 1/26/2005)
Cosponsors (2)

802. H.J.RES.15
Proposing an amendment to the Constitution of the United States to make eligible for the Office of President a person who is not a natural born citizen of the United States but has been a United States citizen for at least 20 years.
Sponsor: Rep Rohrabacher, Dana [R, CA-46] (introduced 2/1/2005)
Cosponsors (None)

803. H.J.RES.16
Proposing an amendment to the Constitution of the United States to repeal the sixteenth article of amendment.
Sponsor: Rep King, Steve [R, IA-5] (introduced 2/1/2005)
Cosponsors (14)

804. H.J.RES.17
Proposing an amendment to the Constitution of the United States to provide for the direct election of the President and Vice President by the popular vote of the citizens of the United States.
Sponsor: Rep Engel, Eliot L. [D, NY-17] (introduced 2/9/2005)
Cosponsors (4)

805. H.J.RES.21
Proposing an amendment to the Constitution of the United States relating to school prayer.
Sponsor: Rep Murtha, John P. [D, PA-12] (introduced 2/16/2005)
Cosponsors (None)

806. H.J.RES.22
Proposing a balanced budget amendment to the Constitution of the United States.
Sponsor: Rep Cooper, Jim [D, TN-5] (introduced 2/17/2005)
Cosponsors (30)

807. H.J.RES.24
Proposing an amendment to the Constitution of the United States to

repeal the 22nd amendment to the Constitution.
Sponsor: Rep Hoyer, Steny H. [D, MD-5] (introduced 2/17/2005)
Cosponsors (4)

808. H.J.RES.25
Proposing an amendment to the Constitution of the United States relating to the maintenance of a system of social insurance that provides social security for its citizens.
Sponsor: Rep Michaud, Michael H. [D, ME-2] (introduced 2/17/2005)
Cosponsors (None)

809. H.J.RES.26
Proposing an amendment to the Constitution of the United States relating to Congressional succession.
Sponsor: Rep Rohrabacher, Dana [R, CA-46] (introduced 2/17/2005)
Cosponsors (1)

810. H.J.RES.28
Proposing an amendment to the Constitution of the United States regarding the right to vote.
Sponsor: Rep Jackson, Jesse L., Jr. [D, IL-2] (introduced 3/2/2005)
Cosponsors (61)

811. H.J.RES.29
Proposing an amendment to the Constitution of the United States regarding the right of all citizens of the United States to a public education of equal high quality.
Sponsor: Rep Jackson, Jesse L., Jr. [D, IL-2] (introduced 3/2/2005)
Cosponsors (35)

812. H.J.RES.30
Proposing an amendment to the Constitution of the United States regarding the right of citizens of the United States to health care of equal high quality.
Sponsor: Rep Jackson, Jesse L., Jr. [D, IL-2] (introduced 3/2/2005)
Cosponsors (35)

813. H.J.RES.31
Proposing an amendment to the Constitution of the United States relating to equality of rights and reproductive rights.
Sponsor: Rep Jackson, Jesse L., Jr. [D, IL-2] (introduced 3/2/2005)
Cosponsors (None)

814. H.J.RES.32
Proposing an amendment to the Constitution of the United States respecting the right to decent, safe, sanitary, and affordable housing.
Sponsor: Rep Jackson, Jesse L., Jr. [D, IL-2] (introduced 3/2/2005)
Cosponsors (None)

815. H.J.RES.33
Proposing an amendment to the Constitution of the United States respecting the right to a clean, safe, and sustainable environment.
Sponsor: Rep Jackson, Jesse L., Jr. [D, IL-2] (introduced 3/2/2005)
Cosponsors (None)

816. H.J.RES.34
Proposing an amendment to the Constitution of the United States relative to taxing the people of the United States progressively.
Sponsor: Rep Jackson, Jesse L., Jr. [D, IL-2] (introduced 3/2/2005)
Cosponsors (None)

817. H.J.RES.35
Proposing an amendment to the Constitution of the United States respecting the right to full employment and balanced growth.
Sponsor: Rep Jackson, Jesse L., Jr. [D, IL-2] (introduced 3/2/2005)
Cosponsors (None)

818. H.J.RES.36
Proposing an amendment to the Constitution of the United States to abolish the Electoral College and provide for the direct election of the President and Vice President by the popular vote of all citizens of the United States regardless of place of residence.
Sponsor: Rep Jackson, Jesse L., Jr. [D, IL-2] (introduced 3/2/2005)
Cosponsors (3)

819. H.J.RES.37
Proposing an amendment to the Constitution of the United States relative to equal rights for men and women.
Sponsor: Rep Maloney, Carolyn B. [D, NY-14] (introduced 3/15/2005)
Cosponsors (185)

820. H.J.RES.39
Proposing an amendment to the Constitution of the United States relating to marriage.

Sponsor: Rep Lungren, Daniel E. [R, CA-3] (introduced 3/17/2005)
Cosponsors (29)

821. H.J.RES.40
Proposing an amendment to the Constitution of the United States respecting the right to a home.
Sponsor: Rep Rangel, Charles B. [D, NY-15] (introduced 4/5/2005)
Cosponsors (None)

822. H.J.RES.41
Proposing an amendment to the Constitution of the United States to provide that no person born in the United States will be a United States citizen unless a parent is a United States citizen, or is lawfully admitted for permanent residence in the United States, at the time of the birth.
Sponsor: Rep Foley, Mark [R, FL-16] (introduced 4/13/2005)
Cosponsors (3)

823. H.J.RES.42
Proposing an amendment to the Constitution of the United States to permit persons who are not natural-born citizens of the United States, but who have been citizens of the United States for at least 35 years, to be eligible to hold the offices of President and Vice President.
Sponsor: Rep Snyder, Vic [D, AR-2] (introduced 4/14/2005)
Cosponsors (1)

824. H.J.RES.43
Proposing an amendment to the Constitution of the United States to establish English as the official language of the United States.
Sponsor: Rep Tancredo, Thomas G. [R, CO-6] (introduced 4/21/2005)
Cosponsors (4)

825. H.J.RES.46
Proposing an amendment to the Constitution of the United States to deny United States citizenship to individuals born in the United States to parents who are neither United States citizens nor persons who owe permanent allegiance to the United States.
Sponsor: Rep Paul, Ron [R, TX-14] (introduced 4/28/2005)
Cosponsors (4)

826. H.J.RES.49
Proposing an amendment to the Constitution of the United States regarding the appointment of individuals to serve as Members of the

House of Representatives when, in a national emergency, a significant number of Members are unable to serve due to death, resignation, or incapacity.

Sponsor: Rep Lofgren, Zoe [D, CA-16] (introduced 5/12/2005)

Cosponsors (None)

827. H.J.RES.50

Proposing an amendment to the Constitution of the United States to abolish the Electoral College and to provide for the direct election of the President and Vice President of the United States.

Sponsor: Rep Lofgren, Zoe [D, CA-16] (introduced 5/12/2005)

Cosponsors (4)

828. H.J.RES.51

Proposing an amendment to the Constitution of the United States to allow debate to be closed on any measure, motion, or other matter pending before the Senate only by unanimous consent or the concurrence of three-fifths of the Senators.

Sponsor: Rep Pallone, Frank, Jr. [D, NJ-6] (introduced 5/23/2005)

Cosponsors (None)

829. H.J.RES.53

Proposing an amendment to the Constitution of the United States to provide that Representatives shall be apportioned among the several States according to their respective numbers, counting the number of persons in each State who are citizens of the United States.

Sponsor: Rep Miller, Candice S. [R, MI-10] (introduced 6/9/2005)

Cosponsors (37)

830. H.J.RES.57

Proposing an amendment to the Constitution of the United States protecting religious freedom.

Sponsor: Rep Istook, Ernest J., Jr. [R, OK-5] (introduced 6/30/2005)

Cosponsors (116)

831. H.J.RES.58

Proposing a balanced budget amendment the Constitution of the United States.

Sponsor: Rep Istook, Ernest J., Jr. [R, OK-5] (introduced 7/13/2005)

Cosponsors (143)

832. H.J.RES.60
Proposing an amendment to the Constitution of the United States relating to the permissible uses for which private property may be taken.
Sponsor: Rep Aderholt, Robert B. [R, AL-4] (introduced 7/14/2005)
Cosponsors (7)

833. H.J.RES.62
Proposing an amendment to the Constitution of the United States to require that Federal district court judges be reconfirmed every ten years by the executive and legislative authorities of the State in which they serve.
Sponsor: Rep Culberson, John Abney [R, TX-7] (introduced 7/28/2005)
Cosponsors (15)

834. H.J.RES.63
Proposing an amendment to the Constitution of the United States to allow an item veto of appropriation bills.
Sponsor: Rep Kennedy, Mark R. [R, MN-6] (introduced 7/29/2005)
Cosponsors (1)

835. H.J.RES.67
Proposing an amendment to the Constitution of the United States to authorize the line item veto.
Sponsor: Rep Platts, Todd Russell [R, PA-19] (introduced 9/21/2005)
Cosponsors (8)

836. H.J.RES.71
Proposing an amendment to the Constitution of the United States to authorize the President to reduce or disapprove any appropriation in any bill presented by Congress.
Sponsor: Rep Kennedy, Mark R. [R, MN-6] (introduced 11/4/2005)
Cosponsors (17)

837. H.J.RES.74
Proposing a balanced budget amendment to the Constitution of the United States.
Sponsor: Rep Jenkins, William L. [R, TN-1] (introduced 12/14/2005)
Cosponsors (None)

838. H.J.RES.76
Proposing an amendment to the Constitution of the United States relating to limitations on the amounts of contributions and expenditures that

may be made in connection with campaigns for election to public office.
Sponsor: Rep Kaptur, Marcy [D, OH-9] (introduced 2/1/2006)
Cosponsors (None)

839. H.J.RES.77
Proposing an amendment to the Constitution of the United States to authorize the President to reduce or disapprove any appropriation or authorization of new direct spending in any bill presented by Congress.
Sponsor: Rep Stearns, Cliff [R, FL-6] (introduced 2/8/2006)
Cosponsors (None)

840. H.J.RES.80
Proposing an amendment the Constitution of the United States limiting the number of consecutive terms that a Senator or Representative may serve and providing for 4-year terms for Representatives.
Sponsor: Rep Owens, Major R. [D, NY-11] (introduced 3/2/2006)
Cosponsors (None)

841. H.J.RES.84
No Taxation Without Representation Amendment
Sponsor: Rep Akin, W. Todd [R, MO-2] (introduced 4/27/2006)
Cosponsors (3)

842. H.J.RES.85
Proposing an amendment to the Constitution of the United States to clarify that the Constitution neither prohibits voluntary prayer nor requires prayer in schools.
Sponsor: Rep Rahall, Nick J., II [D, WV-3] (introduced 5/4/2006)
Cosponsors (1)

843. H.J.RES.88
Marriage Protection Amendment
Sponsor: Rep Musgrave, Marilyn N. [R, CO-4] (introduced 6/6/2006)
Cosponsors (134)

844. H.J.RES.91
Proposing an amendment to the Constitution of the United States relating to marriage.
Sponsor: Rep Gohmert, Louie [R, TX-1] (introduced 7/11/2006)
Cosponsors (None)

845. H.J.RES.92

Proposing an amendment to the Constitution of the United States to ensure a free and adequate education for every child who is a citizen.

Sponsor: Rep Owens, Major R. [D, NY-11] (introduced 7/20/2006)

Cosponsors (None)

846. H.J.RES.98

Proposing a balanced budget amendment to the Constitution of the United States.

Sponsor: Rep Musgrave, Marilyn N. [R, CO-4] (introduced 9/28/2006)

Cosponsors (None)

847. H.J.RES.99

Health Protection Amendment

Sponsor: Rep McCollum, Betty [D, MN-4] (introduced 9/29/2006)

Cosponsors (None)

Senate

848. S.J.RES.1
Marriage Protection Amendment
Sponsor: Sen Allard, Wayne [R, CO] (introduced 1/24/2005)
Cosponsors (32)

849. S.J.RES.2
A joint resolution proposing an amendment to the Constitution of the United States relative to require a balanced budget and protect Social Security surpluses.
Sponsor: Sen Craig, Larry E. [R, ID] (introduced 1/24/2005)
Cosponsors (1)

850. S.J.RES.3
A joint resolution proposing an amendment to the Constitution of the United States relative to limiting the number of terms that a Member of Congress may serve.
Sponsor: Sen Vitter, David [R, LA] (introduced 2/10/2005)
Cosponsors (None)

851. S.J.RES.6
A joint resolution proposing an amendment to the Constitution of the United States to ensure continuity of congressional operations and the avoidance of martial law in the event of mass incapacitations or death in either House of Congress.
Sponsor: Sen Cornyn, John [R, TX] (introduced 2/17/2005)
Cosponsors (1)

852. S.J.RES.7
A joint resolution proposing an amendment to the Constitution of the United States relative to equal rights for men and women.
Sponsor: Sen Kennedy, Edward M. [D, MA] (introduced 3/15/2005)
Cosponsors (20)

853. S.J.RES.10
A joint resolution proposing an amendment to the Constitution of the United States which requires (except during time of war and subject to suspension by Congress) that the total amount of money expended by the United States during any fiscal year not exceed the amount of certain revenue received by the United States during such fiscal year and not ex-

ceed 20 per centum of the gross national product of the United States during the previous calendar year.
Sponsor: Sen Shelby, Richard C. [R, AL] (introduced 3/16/2005)
Cosponsors (1)

854. S.J.RES.11
A joint resolution proposing an amendment to the Constitution of the United States to abolish the electoral college and to provide for the direct popular election of the President and Vice President of the United States.
Sponsor: Sen Feinstein, Dianne [D, CA] (introduced 3/16/2005)
Cosponsors (1)

856. S.J.RES.12
A joint resolution proposing an amendment to the Constitution of the United States authorizing Congress to prohibit the physical desecration of the flag of the United States.
Sponsor: Sen Hatch, Orrin G. [R, UT] (introduced 4/14/2005)
Cosponsors (59)
[Note: A vote on this measure narrowly failed in the Senate on 6/27/2006 by a vote of 66 – 34.]

856. S.J.RES.13
A joint resolution proposing an amendment to the Constitution of the United States relative to marriage.
Sponsor: Sen Brownback, Sam [R, KS] (introduced 4/14/2005)
Cosponsors (1)

857. S.J.RES.24
A joint resolution proposing an amendment to the Constitution of the United States relative to the reference to God in the Pledge of Allegiance and on United States currency.
Sponsor: Sen Landrieu, Mary L. [D, LA] (introduced 9/14/2005)
Cosponsors (None)

858. S.J.RES.25
A joint resolution proposing an amendment to the Constitution of the United States to authorize the President to reduce or disapprove any appropriation in any bill presented by Congress.
Sponsor: Sen Talent, Jim [R, MO] (introduced 9/27/2005)
Cosponsors (11)

859. S.J.RES.26
A joint resolution proposing an amendment to the Constitution of the United States relative to the line item veto.
Sponsor: Sen Dole, Elizabeth [R, NC] (introduced 9/27/2005)
Cosponsors (None)

860. S.J.RES.31
A joint resolution proposing an amendment to the Constitution of the United States relative to require a balancing of the budget.
Sponsor: Sen Allen, George [R, VA] (introduced 2/15/2006)
Cosponsors (None)

861. S.J.RES.35
A joint resolution proposing an amendment to the Constitution of the United States to clarify that the Constitution neither prohibits voluntary prayer nor requires prayer in schools.
Sponsor: Sen Byrd, Robert C. [D, WV] (introduced 4/27/2006)
Cosponsors (6)

110th Congress (2007-2008)

House

862. H.J.RES.1
Proposing a balanced budget amendment to the Constitution of the United States.
Sponsor: Rep Goodlatte, Bob [R, VA-6] (introduced 1/4/2007)
Cosponsors (163)

863. H.J.RES.2
Proposing an amendment the Constitution of the United States regarding presidential election voting rights for residents of all United States territories and commonwealths.
Sponsor: Rep Christensen, Donna M. [D, VI] (introduced 1/4/2007)
Cosponsors (1)

864. H.J.RES.4
Every Vote Counts Amendment
Sponsor: Rep Green, Gene [D, TX-29] (introduced 1/4/2007)
Cosponsors (2)

865. H.J.RES.5
Proposing an amendment to the Constitution of the United States relating to limitations on the amounts of contributions and expenditures that may be made in connection with campaigns for election to public office.
Sponsor: Rep Kaptur, Marcy [D, OH-9] (introduced 1/4/2007)
Cosponsors (1)

866. H.J.RES.6
Proposing an amendment to the Constitution of the United States to provide that Representatives shall be apportioned among the several States according to their respective numbers, counting the number of persons in each State who are citizens of the United States.
Sponsor: Rep Miller, Candice S. [R, MI-10] (introduced 1/4/2007)
Cosponsors (31)

967. H.J.RES.7

Proposing a balanced budget amendment to the Constitution of the United States.

Sponsor: Rep Musgrave, Marilyn N. [R, CO-4] (introduced 1/4/2007)

Cosponsors (1)

868. H.J.RES.8

Proposing an amendment to the Constitution of the United States to repeal the twenty-second article of amendment, thereby removing the limitation on the number of terms an individual may serve as President.

Sponsor: Rep Serrano, Jose E. [D, NY-16] (introduced 1/4/2007)

Cosponsors (None)

869. H.J.RES.9

Proposing an amendment to the Constitution of the United States authorizing the Congress and the States to prohibit the act of desecration of the flag of the United States and to set criminal penalties for that act.

Sponsor: Rep Emerson, Jo Ann [R, MO-8] (introduced 1/5/2007)

Cosponsors (28)

870. H.J.RES.10

Proposing an amendment to the Constitution to provide for a balanced budget for the United States Government and for greater accountability in the enactment of tax legislation.

Sponsor: Rep Emerson, Jo Ann [R, MO-8] (introduced 1/5/2007)

Cosponsors (None)

871. H.J.RES.11

Proposing an amendment to the Constitution of the United States relating to voluntary school prayer.

Sponsor: Rep Emerson, Jo Ann [R, MO-8] (introduced 1/5/2007)

Cosponsors (1)

872. H.J.RES.12

Proposing an amendment to the Constitution of the United States authorizing the Congress to prohibit the physical desecration of the flag of the United States.

Sponsor: Rep Murtha, John P. [D, PA-12] (introduced 1/11/2007)

Cosponsors (72)

873. H.J.RES.13
Proposing an amendment to the Constitution of the United States relating to school prayer.
Sponsor: Rep Murtha, John P. [D, PA-12] (introduced 1/11/2007)
Cosponsors (None)

874. H.J.RES.16
Proposing an amendment to the Constitution of the United States to repeal the sixteenth article of amendment.
Sponsor: Rep King, Steve [R, IA-5] (introduced 1/17/2007)
Cosponsors (6)

875. H.J.RES.17
Proposing an amendment to the Constitution of the United States establishing English as the official language of the United States.
Sponsor: Rep Doolittle, John T. [R, CA-4] (introduced 1/17/2007)
Cosponsors (None)

876. H.J.RES.19
Proposing an amendment to the Constitution of the United States to establish English as the official language of the United States.
Sponsor: Rep Tancredo, Thomas G. [R, CO-6] (introduced 1/18/2007)
Cosponsors (5)

877. H.J.RES.21
Proposing a balanced budget amendment to the Constitution of the United States.
Sponsor: Rep Buchanan, Vern [R, FL-13] (introduced 1/31/2007)
Cosponsors (6)

878. H.J.RES.22
Proposing an amendment to the Constitution of the United States relating to marriage.
Sponsor: Rep Lungren, Daniel E. [R, CA-3] (introduced 2/6/2007)
Cosponsors (46)

879. H.J.RES.23
Proposing an amendment the Constitution of the United States relative to abolishing personal income, estate, and gift taxes and prohibiting the United States Government from engaging in business in competition with its citizens.

Sponsor: Rep Paul, Ron [R, TX-14] (introduced 2/7/2007)
Cosponsors (4)

880. H.J.RES.24
Proposing an amendment to the Constitution of the United States to limit the number of consecutive terms that a Member of Congress may serve.
Sponsor: Rep Platts, Todd Russell [R, PA-19] (introduced 2/8/2007)
Cosponsors (None)

881. H.J.RES.28
Proposing an amendment to the Constitution of the United States regarding the right to vote.
Sponsor: Rep Jackson, Jesse L., Jr. [D, IL-2] (introduced 2/13/2007)
Cosponsors (51)

882. H.J.RES.29
Proposing an amendment to the Constitution of the United States regarding the right of all citizens of the United States to a public education of equal high quality.
Sponsor: Rep Jackson, Jesse L., Jr. [D, IL-2] (introduced 2/13/2007)
Cosponsors (None)

883. H.J.RES.30
Proposing an amendment to the Constitution of the United States regarding the right of citizens of the United States to health care of equal high quality.
Sponsor: Rep Jackson, Jesse L., Jr. [D, IL-2] (introduced 2/13/2007)
Cosponsors (3)

884. H.J.RES.31
Proposing an amendment to the Constitution of the United States relating to equality of rights and reproductive rights.
Sponsor: Rep Jackson, Jesse L., Jr. [D, IL-2] (introduced 2/13/2007)
Cosponsors (None)

885. H.J.RES.32
Proposing an amendment to the Constitution of the United States respecting the right to decent, safe, sanitary, and affordable housing.
Sponsor: Rep Jackson, Jesse L., Jr. [D, IL-2] (introduced 2/13/2007)
Cosponsors (None)

886. H.J.RES.33
Proposing an amendment the Constitution of the United States respecting the right to a clean, safe, and sustainable environment.
Sponsor: Rep Jackson, Jesse L., Jr. [D, IL-2] (introduced 2/13/2007)
Cosponsors (None)

887. H.J.RES.34
Proposing an amendment to the Constitution of the United States relative to taxing the people of the United States progressively.
Sponsor: Rep Jackson, Jesse L., Jr. [D, IL-2] (introduced 2/13/2007)
Cosponsors (None)

888. H.J.RES.35
Proposing an amendment to the Constitution of the United States respecting the right to full employment and balanced growth.
Sponsor: Rep Jackson, Jesse L., Jr. [D, IL-2] (introduced 2/13/2007)
Cosponsors (1)

889. H.J.RES.36
Proposing an amendment to the Constitution of the United States to abolish the Electoral College and provide for the direct election of the President and Vice President by the popular vote of all citizens of the United States regardless of place of residence.
Sponsor: Rep Jackson, Jesse L., Jr. [D, IL-2] (introduced 2/13/2007)
Cosponsors (2)

890. H.J.RES.38
Proposing an amendment to the Constitution of the United States to authorize the line item veto.
Sponsor: Rep Platts, Todd Russell [R, PA-19] (introduced 2/27/2007)
Cosponsors (None)

891. H.J.RES.40
Proposing an amendment to the Constitution of the United States relative to equal rights for men and women.
Sponsor: Rep Maloney, Carolyn B. [D, NY-14] (introduced 3/27/2007)
Cosponsors (204)

892. H.J.RES.41
Proposing an amendment to the Constitution of the United States to clarify that the Constitution neither prohibits voluntary prayer nor re-

quires prayer in schools.
Sponsor: Rep Rahall, Nick J., II [D, WV-3] (introduced 3/29/2007)
Cosponsors (None)

893. H.J.RES.45

Proposing a balanced budget amendment to the Constitution of the United States.
Sponsor: Rep Gillibrand, Kirsten E. [D, NY-20] (introduced 6/12/2007)
Cosponsors (32)

894. H.J.RES.46

Proposing an amendment to the Constitution of the United States to deny United States citizenship to individuals born in the United States to parents who are neither United States citizens nor persons who owe permanent allegiance to the United States.
Sponsor: Rep Paul, Ron [R, TX-14] (introduced 6/13/2007)
Cosponsors (7)

895. H.J.RES.48

Proposing an amendment to the Constitution of the United States regarding the requirement of the approval of a two-thirds majority of the Supreme Court for any pardon or reprieve granted by the President.
Sponsor: Rep Cohen, Steve [D, TN-9] (introduced 8/3/2007)
Cosponsors (2)

896. H.J.RES.56

Proposing an amendment to the Constitution of the United States to temporarily fill mass vacancies in the House of Representatives and the Senate and to preserve the right of the people to elect their Representatives and Senators in Congress.
Sponsor: Rep Baird, Brian [D, WA-3] (introduced 10/4/2007)
Cosponsors (1)

897. H.J.RES.57

Proposing an amendment to the Constitution of the United States relating to Congressional succession.
Sponsor: Rep Rohrabacher, Dana [R, CA-46] (introduced 10/4/2007)
Cosponsors (1)

898. H.J.RES.60

Proposing an amendment to the Constitution of the United States providing for Representatives to be chosen every four years, and to limit the

number of times Senators and Representatives may be elected.
Sponsor: Rep Goode, Virgil H., Jr. [R, VA-5] (introduced 10/24/2007)
Cosponsors (None)

899. H.J.RES.61
Proposing an amendment to the Constitution of the United States relating to contributions and expenditures intended to affect elections.
Sponsor: Rep Higgins, Brian [D, NY-27] (introduced 10/31/2007)
Cosponsors (1)

900. H.J.RES.63
Proposing an amendment to the Constitution of the United States authorizing the President to disapprove or reduce items of appropriation.
Sponsor: Rep English, Phil [R, PA-3] (introduced 11/13/2007)
Cosponsors (1)

901. H.J.RES.66
Proposing an amendment to the Constitution of the United States to establish and protect the rights of victims of violent crimes.
Sponsor: Rep Chabot, Steve [R, OH-1] (introduced 12/6/2007)
Cosponsors (None)

902. H.J.RES.71
Proposing an amendment to the Constitution of the United States to limit the number of years Representatives and Senators may serve.
Sponsor: Rep Price, Tom [R, GA-6] (introduced 12/18/2007)
Cosponsors (None)

903. H.J.RES.73
Proposing an amendment to the Constitution of the United States relating to the process by which the House of Representatives chooses the President of the United States in the event no candidate receives a majority of the electoral votes.
Sponsor: Rep Sherman, Brad [D, CA-27] (introduced 12/18/2007)
Cosponsors (None)

904. H.J.RES.74
Proposing an amendment to the Constitution of the United States relating to marriage.
Sponsor: Rep Gohmert, Louie [R, TX-1] (introduced 12/19/2007)
Cosponsors (None)

905. H.J.RES.75

Proposing an amendment to the Constitution of the United States relating to the process by which the House of Representatives selects the President in the event no candidate receives a majority of electoral votes.
Sponsor: Rep Goode, Virgil H., Jr. [R, VA-5] (introduced 12/19/2007)
Cosponsors (None)

906. H.J.RES.80

Proposing an amendment to the Constitution of the United States prohibiting the penalty of death.
Sponsor: Rep McCollum, Betty [D, MN-4] (introduced 4/16/2008)
Cosponsors (4)

907. H.J.RES.81

Proposing an amendment to the Constitution of the United States to control spending.
Sponsor: Rep Campbell, John [R, CA-48] (introduced 4/30/2008)
Cosponsors (38)

908. H.J.RES.82

Proposing an amendment to the Constitution of the United States allowing castration after conviction for the rape of a child under 16 years of age.
Sponsor: Rep Broun, Paul C. [R, GA-10] (introduced 5/8/2008)
Cosponsors (None)

909. H.J.RES.83

Proposing an amendment to the Constitution of the United States providing that the Constitution does not preclude a penalty of death, including when it is imposed for the rape of a child under 16 years of age.
Sponsor: Rep Broun, Paul C. [R, GA-10] (introduced 5/8/2008)
Cosponsors (None)

910. H.J.RES.89

Proposing an amendment to the Constitution of the United States relating to marriage.
Sponsor: Rep Broun, Paul C. [R, GA-10] (introduced 5/22/2008)
Cosponsors (91)

911. H.J.RES.96

Proposing an amendment to the Constitution of the United States to

permit the penalty of death for the rape of a child.
Sponsor: Rep Chabot, Steve [R, OH-1] (introduced 6/26/2008)
Cosponsors (15)

912. H.J.RES.97

Proposing an amendment to the Constitution of the United States relating to parental rights.
Sponsor: Rep Hoekstra, Peter [R, MI-2] (introduced 6/26/2008)
Cosponsors (None)

913. H.J.RES.98

Proposing an amendment to the Constitution of the United States to limit the number of times Senators and Representatives may be elected.
Sponsor: Rep Kuhl, John R. "Randy", Jr. [R, NY-29] (introduced 9/18/2008)
Cosponsors (None)

914. H.J.RES.99

Proposing an amendment to the Constitution of the United States concerning the election of the Members of the House of Representatives.
Sponsor: Rep Larson, John B. [D, CT-1] (introduced 9/24/2008)
Cosponsors (None)

Senate

915. S.J.RES.1
A joint resolution proposing an amendment to the Constitution of the United States relative to require a balanced budget and protect Social Security surpluses.
Sponsor: Sen Craig, Larry E. [R, ID] (introduced 1/4/2007)
Cosponsors (1)

916. S.J.RES.2
A joint resolution proposing an amendment to the Constitution of the United States relative to limiting the number of terms that a Member of Congress may serve.
Sponsor: Sen Vitter, David [R, LA] (introduced 1/12/2007)
Cosponsors (1)

917. S.J.RES.10
A joint resolution proposing an amendment to the Constitution of the United States relative to equal rights for men and women.
Sponsor: Sen Kennedy, Edward M. [D, MA] (introduced 3/27/2007)
Cosponsors (24)

918. S.J.RES.11
A joint resolution proposing an amendment to the Constitution of the United States to clarify that the Constitution neither prohibits voluntary prayer nor requires prayer in schools.
Sponsor: Sen Byrd, Robert C. [D, WV] (introduced 3/29/2007)
Cosponsors (7)

919. S.J.RES.19
A joint resolution proposing an amendment to the Constitution of the United States relative to Proposing an amendment to the Constitution of the United States which requires (except during time of war and subject to suspension by Congress) that the total amount of money expended by the United States during any fiscal year not exceed the amount of certain revenue received by the United States during such fiscal year and not exceed 20 per centum of the gross national product of the United States during the previous calendar year.
Sponsor: Sen Shelby, Richard C. [R, AL] (introduced 10/1/2007)
Cosponsors (None)

920. S.J.RES.21
A joint resolution proposing an amendment to the Constitution of the United States relating to contributions and expenditures intended to affect elections.
Sponsor: Sen Schumer, Charles E. [D, NY] (introduced 10/18/2007)
Cosponsors (3)

921. S.J.RES.24
A joint resolution proposing a balanced budget amendment to the Constitution of the United States.
Sponsor: Sen Graham, Lindsey [R, SC] (introduced 11/13/2007)
Cosponsors (3)

922. S.J.RES.27
A joint resolution proposing an amendment to the Constitution of the United States relative to the line item veto.
Sponsor: Sen Dole, Elizabeth [R, NC] (introduced 12/11/2007)
Cosponsors (7)

923. S.J.RES.31
A joint resolution proposing an amendment to the Constitution of the United States relating to United States citizenship.
Sponsor: Sen Vitter, David [R, LA] (introduced 4/9/2008)
Cosponsors (None)

924. S.J.RES.39
A joint resolution proposing an amendment to the Constitution of the United States to abolish the electoral college and to provide for the direct popular election of the President and Vice President of the United States.
Sponsor: Sen Nelson, Bill [D, FL] (introduced 6/6/2008)
Cosponsors (None)

925. S.J.RES.40
A joint resolution proposing an amendment to the Constitution of the United States authorizing the Congress and the States to prohibit the act of desecration of the flag of the United States and to set criminal penalties for that act.
Sponsor: Sen Vitter, David [R, LA] (introduced 6/12/2008)
Cosponsors (None)

926. S.J.RES.43

A joint resolution proposing an amendment to the Constitution of the United States relating to marriage.

Sponsor: Sen Wicker, Roger F. [R, MS] (introduced 6/25/2008)

Cosponsors (17)

111th Congress (2009-2010)

House

927. H.J.RES.1
Proposing a balanced budget amendment to the Constitution of the United States.
Sponsor: Rep Goodlatte, Bob [R, VA-6] (introduced 1/6/2009)
Cosponsors (179)

928. H.J.RES.2
Proposing an amendment to the Constitution of the United States regarding presidential election voting rights for residents of all United States territories and commonwealths.
Sponsor: Rep Christensen, Donna M. [D, VI] (introduced 1/6/2009)
Cosponsors (2)

929. H.J.RES.4
Health Protection Amendment of 2009
Sponsor: Rep McCollum, Betty [D, MN-4] (introduced 1/6/2009)
Cosponsors (None)

930. H.J.RES.5
Proposing an amendment to the Constitution of the United States to repeal the twenty-second article of amendment, thereby removing the limitation on the number of terms an individual may serve as President.
Sponsor: Rep Serrano, Jose E. [D, NY-16] (introduced 1/6/2009)
Cosponsors (None)

931. H.J.RES.6
Proposing an amendment to the Constitution of the United States relating to voluntary school prayer.
Sponsor: Rep Emerson, Jo Ann [R, MO-8] (introduced 1/7/2009)
Cosponsors (None)

932. H.J.RES.7
Proposing an amendment to the Constitution to provide for a balanced budget for the United States Government and for greater accountability

in the enactment of tax legislation.
Sponsor: Rep Emerson, Jo Ann [R, MO-8] (introduced 1/7/2009)
Cosponsors (None)

933. H.J.RES.8
Proposing an amendment to the Constitution of the United States authorizing the Congress and the States to prohibit the act of desecration of the flag of the United States and to set criminal penalties for that act.
Sponsor: Rep Emerson, Jo Ann [R, MO-8] (introduced 1/7/2009)
Cosponsors (2)

934. H.J.RES.9
Every Vote Counts Amendment
Sponsor: Rep Green, Gene [D, TX-29] (introduced 1/7/2009)
Cosponsors (None)

935. H.J.RES.11
Proposing an amendment to the Constitution of the United States to provide that Representatives shall be apportioned among the several States according to their respective numbers, counting the number of persons in each State who are citizens of the United States.
Sponsor: Rep Miller, Candice S. [R, MI-10] (introduced 1/7/2009)
Cosponsors (28)

936. H.J.RES.13
Proposing an amendment to the Constitution of the United States relating to limitations on the amounts of contributions and expenditures that may be made in connection with campaigns for election to public office.
Sponsor: Rep Kaptur, Marcy [D, OH-9] (introduced 1/8/2009)
Cosponsors (6)

937. H.J.RES.14
Proposing an amendment to the Constitution of the United States to limit the number of consecutive terms that a Member of Congress may serve.
Sponsor: Rep Platts, Todd Russell [R, PA-19] (introduced 1/8/2009)
Cosponsors (4)

938. H.J.RES.15
Proposing an amendment to the Constitution of the United States to authorize the line item veto.

Sponsor: Rep Platts, Todd Russell [R, PA-19] (introduced 1/8/2009)
Cosponsors (None)

939. H.J.RES.16
Proposing an amendment to the Constitution of the United States to repeal the sixteenth article of amendment.
Sponsor: Rep King, Steve [R, IA-5] (introduced 1/8/2009)
Cosponsors (1)

940. H.J.RES.21
Proposing an amendment to the Constitution of the United States relative to the election of Senators.
Sponsor: Rep Dreier, David [R, CA-26] (introduced 2/11/2009)
Cosponsors (8)

941. H.J.RES.28
Proposing an amendment to the Constitution of the United States regarding the right to vote.
Sponsor: Rep Jackson, Jesse L., Jr. [D, IL-2] (introduced 3/3/2009)
Cosponsors (None)

942. H.J.RES.29
Proposing an amendment to the Constitution of the United States regarding the right of all citizens of the United States to a public education of equal high quality.
Sponsor: Rep Jackson, Jesse L., Jr. [D, IL-2] (introduced 3/3/2009)
Cosponsors (None)

943 H.J.RES.30
Proposing an amendment to the Constitution of the United States regarding the right of citizens of the United States to health care of equal high quality.
Sponsor: Rep Jackson, Jesse L., Jr. [D, IL-2] (introduced 3/3/2009)
Cosponsors (None)

944. H.J.RES.31
Proposing an amendment to the Constitution of the United States relating to equality of rights and reproductive rights.
Sponsor: Rep Jackson, Jesse L., Jr. [D, IL-2] (introduced 3/3/2009)
Cosponsors (None)

945. H.J.RES.32
Proposing an amendment to the Constitution of the United States respecting the right to decent, safe, sanitary, and affordable housing.
Sponsor: Rep Jackson, Jesse L., Jr. [D, IL-2] (introduced 3/3/2009)
Cosponsors (None)

946. H.J.RES.33
Proposing an amendment the Constitution of the United States respecting the right to a clean, safe, and sustainable environment.
Sponsor: Rep Jackson, Jesse L., Jr. [D, IL-2] (introduced 3/3/2009)
Cosponsors (None)

947. H.J.RES.34
Proposing an amendment to the Constitution of the United States relative to taxing the people of the United States progressively.
Sponsor: Rep Jackson, Jesse L., Jr. [D, IL-2] (introduced 3/3/2009)
Cosponsors (None)

948. H.J.RES.35
Proposing an amendment to the Constitution of the United States respecting the right to full employment and balanced growth.
Sponsor: Rep Jackson, Jesse L., Jr. [D, IL-2] (introduced 3/3/2009)
Cosponsors (None)

949. H.J.RES.36
Proposing an amendment to the Constitution of the United States to abolish the Electoral College and provide for the direct election of the President and Vice President by the popular vote of all citizens of the United States regardless of place of residence.
Sponsor: Rep Jackson, Jesse L., Jr. [D, IL-2] (introduced 3/3/2009)
Cosponsors (None)

950. H.J.RES.37
Proposing an amendment to the Constitution of the United States relating to marriage.
Sponsor: Rep Lungren, Daniel E. [R, CA-3] (introduced 3/4/2009)
Cosponsors (41)

951. H.J.RES.41
Proposing an amendment to the Constitution of the United States to prohibit the President from entering into a treaty or other international

agreement that would provide for the United States to adopt as legal tender in the United States a currency issued by an entity other than the United States.
Sponsor: Rep Bachmann, Michele [R, MN-6] (introduced 3/25/2009)
Cosponsors (38)

952. H.J.RES.42

Proposing an amendment to the Constitution of the United States relating to parental rights.
Sponsor: Rep Hoekstra, Peter [R, MI-2] (introduced 3/31/2009)
Cosponsors (141)

953. H.J.RES.43

Proposing a balanced budget amendment to the Constitution of the United States.
Sponsor: Rep Buchanan, Vern [R, FL-13] (introduced 4/22/2009)
Cosponsors (1)

954. H.J.RES.47

Proposing an amendment to the Constitution of the United States giving Congress power to prohibit the physical desecration of the flag of the United States.
Sponsor: Rep Emerson, Jo Ann [R, MO-8] (introduced 4/30/2009)
Cosponsors (84)

955. H.J.RES.48

Proposing an amendment to the Constitution of the United States relative to abolishing personal income, estate, and gift taxes and prohibiting the United States Government from engaging in business in competition with its citizens.
Sponsor: Rep Paul, Ron [R, TX-14] (introduced 4/30/2009)
Cosponsors (2)

956. H.J.RES.49

Proposing an amendment to the Constitution of the United States concerning the election of the Members of the House of Representatives.
Sponsor: Rep Larson, John B. [D, CT-1] (introduced 5/5/2009)
Cosponsors (None)

957. H.J.RES.50

Proposing an amendment to the Constitution of the United States relat-

ing to marriage.
Sponsor: Rep Broun, Paul C. [R, GA-10] (introduced 5/7/2009)
Cosponsors (43)

958. H.J.RES.51
Proposing an amendment to the Constitution of the United States to permit the penalty of death for the rape of a child.
Sponsor: Rep Gohmert, Louie [R, TX-1] (introduced 5/7/2009)
Cosponsors (14)

959. H.J.RES.52
Proposing an amendment to the Constitution of the United States to temporarily fill mass vacancies in the House of Representatives and the Senate and to preserve the right of the people to elect their Representatives and Senators in Congress.
Sponsor: Rep Baird, Brian [D, WA-3] (introduced 5/20/2009)
Cosponsors (1)

960. H.J.RES.53
Proposing an amendment to the Constitution of the United States relating to Congressional succession.
Sponsor: Rep Rohrabacher, Dana [R, CA-46] (introduced 5/20/2009)
Cosponsors (1)

961. H.J.RES.57
Preserving Capitalism in America Amendment
Sponsor: Rep Turner, Michael R. [R, OH-3] (introduced 6/23/2009)
Cosponsors (104)

962. H.J.RES.59
Proposing an amendment to the Constitution of the United States to protect the rights of crime victims.
Sponsor: Rep Stupak, Bart [D, MI-1] (introduced 7/9/2009)
Cosponsors (1)

963. H.J.RES.61
Proposing an amendment to the Constitution of the United States relative to equal rights for men and women.
Sponsor: Rep Maloney, Carolyn B. [D, NY-14] (introduced 7/21/2009)
Cosponsors (84)

964. H.J.RES.63
Proposing an amendment to the Constitution of the United States to limit the number of years Representatives and Senators may serve.
Sponsor: Rep Price, Tom [R, GA-6] (introduced 12/14/2009)
Cosponsors (1)

965. H.J.RES.67
Proposing an amendment to the Constitution of the United States to limit the number of consecutive terms that a Member of Congress may serve.
Sponsor: Rep Hall, Ralph M. [R, TX-4] (introduced 1/21/2010)
Cosponsors (2)

966. H.J.RES.68
Proposing an amendment to the Constitution of the United States prohibiting corporations and labor organizations from using operating funds for advertisements in connection with any campaign for election for Federal office.
Sponsor: Rep Boswell, Leonard L. [D, IA-3] (introduced 1/21/2010)
Cosponsors (None)

967. H.J.RES.69
Proposing an amendment to the Constitution of the United States to give citizens of the United States the right to enact and repeal laws by voting on legislation in a national election.
Sponsor: Rep Hoekstra, Peter [R, MI-2] (introduced 1/21/2010)
Cosponsors (None)

968. H.J.RES.70
Proposing an amendment to the Constitution of the United States to give citizens of the United States the right to propose amendments to the Constitution by an initiative process.
Sponsor: Rep Hoekstra, Peter [R, MI-2] (introduced 1/21/2010)
Cosponsors (None)

969. H.J.RES.71
Proposing an amendment to the Constitution of the United States to give citizens of the United States the right to recall elected officials.
Sponsor: Rep Hoekstra, Peter [R, MI-2] (introduced 1/21/2010)
Cosponsors (None)

970. H.J.RES.73
Proposing an amendment to the Constitution of the United States to balance the Federal budget.
Sponsor: Rep Broun, Paul C. [R, GA-10] (introduced 1/27/2010)
Cosponsors (9)

971. H.J.RES.74
Proposing an amendment to the Constitution of the United States permitting Congress and the States to regulate the expenditure of funds by corporations engaging in political speech.
Sponsor: Rep Edwards, Donna F. [D, MD-4] (introduced 2/2/2010)
Cosponsors (26)

972. H.J.RES.75
Proposing an amendment to the Constitution of the United States to balance the Federal budget.
Sponsor: Rep Broun, Paul C. [R, GA-10] (introduced 2/3/2010)
Cosponsors (11)

973. H.J.RES.78
Proposing a balanced budget amendment to the Constitution of the United States.
Sponsor: Rep Bright, Bobby [D, AL-2] (introduced 3/2/2010)
Cosponsors (42)

974. H.J.RES.79
Proposing an amendment to the Constitution of the United States to control spending.
Sponsor: Rep Hensarling, Jeb [R, TX-5] (introduced 3/3/2010)
Cosponsors (53)

975. H.J.RES.82
Proposing the "Doris 'Granny D' Haddock Amendment of 2010" to the Constitution of the United States regarding the authority of Congress and the States to regulate the spending and activities of corporations with regard to political campaigns and campaigns for election for public office.
Sponsor: Rep Hodes, Paul W. [D, NH-2] (introduced 4/14/2010)
Cosponsors (None)

976. H.J.RES.84

Proposing an amendment to the Constitution of the United States giving Congress power to regulate campaign contributions for Federal elections.

Sponsor: Rep Schrader, Kurt [D, OR-5] (introduced 5/13/2010)

Cosponsors (None)

977. H.J.RES.87

Proposing an amendment to the Constitution of the United States.

Sponsor: Rep Neugebauer, Randy [R, TX-19] (introduced 5/26/2010)

Cosponsors (19)

978. H.J.RES.89

Proposing a balanced budget amendment to the Constitution of the United States.

Sponsor: Rep Terry, Lee [R, NE-2] (introduced 6/16/2010)

Cosponsors (None)

979. H.J.RES.95

Proposing an amendment to the Constitution of the United States allowing the States to call a limited convention solely for the purposes of considering whether to propose a specific amendment to the Constitution.

Sponsor: Rep Minnick, Walter [D, ID-1] (introduced 7/30/2010)

Cosponsors (4)

980. H.J.RES.98

Proposing an amendment to the Constitution of the United States authorizing regulation of any expenditure in connection to an election.

Sponsor: Rep Deutch, Theodore E. [D, FL-19] (introduced 9/29/2010)

Cosponsors (None)

981. H.J. RES. 102

Proposing an Amendment to the Constitution of the United States to give States the right to repeal Federal laws and regulations when ratified by the Legislatures of two thirds of the Several States.

Sponsor: Rep Bishop, Rob [UT-1] (introduced 11/30/2010)

Cosponsors (1)

982. H.J.RES. 106

Proposing an Amendment to the Constitution of the United States re-

lating to the use of foreign law as authority in Federal courts.
Sponsor: Rep Culberson, John Abney (R, TDX-7) (Introduced 12/22-2010)

Cosponsors (None)

983. H.J.RES. 107
Proposing an amendment to the Constitution of the United States regarding the effect of treaties, Executive orders, and agreements with other nations or groups of nations.
Sonsor: Rep Culberson, John Abney (R, TX-7) (introduced 12/22/2010).

Cosponsors (None)

Senate

984 S.J.RES.1
A joint resolution proposing an amendment to the Constitution of the United States relative to limiting the number of terms that a Member of Congress may serve.
Sponsor: Sen Vitter, David [R, LA] (introduced 1/6/2009)
Cosponsors (3)

985. S.J.RES.2
A joint resolution proposing an amendment to the Constitution of the United States authorizing the Congress and the States to prohibit the act of desecration of the flag of the United States and to set criminal penalties for that act.
Sponsor: Sen Vitter, David [R, LA] (introduced 1/6/2009)
Cosponsors (None)

986. S.J.RES.4
A joint resolution proposing an amendment to the Constitution of the United States to abolish the electoral college and to provide for the direct popular election of the President and Vice President of the United States.
Sponsor: Sen Nelson, Bill [D, FL] (introduced 1/8/2009)
Cosponsors (None)

987. S.J.RES.6
A joint resolution proposing an amendment to the Constitution of the United States relating to United States citizenship.
Sponsor: Sen Vitter, David [R, LA] (introduced 1/16/2009)
Cosponsors (None)

988. S.J.RES.7
A joint resolution proposing an amendment to the Constitution of the United States relative to the election of Senators.
Sponsor: Sen Feingold, Russell D. [D, WI] (introduced 1/29/2009)
Cosponsors (3)

989. S.J.RES.11
A joint resolution proposing an amendment to the Constitution of the United States relative to a seat in the House of Representatives for the District of Columbia.

Sponsor: Sen Murkowski, Lisa [R, AK] (introduced 2/25/2009)
Cosponsors (1)

990. S.J.RES.13
A joint resolution proposing an amendment to the Constitution of the United States relative to parental rights.
Sponsor: Sen Vitter, David [R, LA] (introduced 3/3/2009)
Cosponsors (None)

991. S.J.RES.15
A joint resolution proposing an amendment to the Constitution of the United States authorizing the Congress to prohibit the physical desecration of the flag of the United States.
Sponsor: Sen Vitter, David [R, LA] (introduced 5/6/2009)
Cosponsors (26)

992. S.J.RES.16
A joint resolution proposing an amendment to the Constitution of the United States relative to parental rights.
Sponsor: Sen DeMint, Jim [R, SC] (introduced 5/14/2009)
Cosponsors (6)

993. S.J.RES.20
A joint resolution proposing an amendment to the Constitution of the United States which requires (except during time of war and subject to suspension by Congress) that the total amount of money expended by the United States during any fiscal year not exceed the amount of certain revenue received by the United States during such fiscal year and not exceed 20 per cent of the gross national product of the United States during the previous calendar year.
Sponsor: Sen Shelby, Richard C. [R, AL] (introduced 10/1/2009)
Cosponsors (2)

994. S.J.RES.21
A joint resolution proposing an amendment to the Constitution of the United States relative to limiting the number of terms that a Member of Congress may serve to 3 in the House of Representatives and 2 in the Senate.
Sponsor: Sen DeMint, Jim [R, SC] (introduced 11/10/2009)
Cosponsors (3)

995. S.J.RES.22

A joint resolution proposing an amendment to the Constitution of the United States relative to requiring a balanced budget and granting the President of the United States the power of line-item veto.

Sponsor: Sen LeMieux, George S. [R, FL] (introduced 12/15/2009)

Cosponsors (1)

996. S.J.RES.27

A joint resolution proposing a balanced budget amendment to the Constitution of the United States.

Sponsor: Sen DeMint, Jim [R, SC] (introduced 2/4/2010)

Cosponsors (16)

997. S.J.RES.28

A joint resolution proposing an amendment to the Constitution of the United States relating to contributions and expenditures intended to affect elections.

Sponsor: Sen Dodd, Christopher J. [D, CT] (introduced 2/24/2010)

Cosponsors (3)

998. S.J.RES.35

A joint resolution proposing an amendment to the Constitution of the United States relative to a balanced budget.

Sponsor: Sen Hatch, Orrin G. [R, UT] (introduced 7/21/2010)

Cosponsors (None)

999. S.J.RES.36

A joint resolution proposing an amendment to the Constitution of the United States relative to authorizing regulation of contributions to candidates for State public office and Federal office by corporations and labor organizations, and expenditures by corporate entities and labor organizations in support of, or opposition to such candidates.

Sponsor: Sen Baucus, Max [D, MT] (introduced 7/27/2010)

Cosponsors (None)

1000. S.J.RES.38

A joint resolution proposing a balanced budget amendment to the Constitution of the United States.

Sponsor: Sen DeMint, Jim [R, SC] (introduced 8/3/2010)

Cosponsors (None)

1001. S.J.RES.41
A joint resolution proposing an amendment to the Constitution of the United States relative to equal rights for men and women.
Sponsor: Sen Menendez, Robert [D, NJ] (introduced 12/10/2010)
Cosponsors (7)

112th Congress (2011-2012)

House

1002. H.J.RES.1
Proposing a balanced budget amendment to the Constitution of the United States.
Sponsor: Rep. Goodlatte, Bob [R-VA-6] (Introduced 01/05/2011)
Cosponsors (133)

1003. H.J.RES.2
Proposing a balanced budget amendment to the Constitution of the United States.
Sponsor: Rep. Goodlatte, Bob [R-VA-6] (Introduced 01/05/2011)
Cosponsors (242)

1004. H.J.RES.3
Proposing an amendment to the Constitution of the United States relating to parental rights.
Sponsor: Rep. Fleming, John [R-LA-4] (Introduced 01/05/2011)
Cosponsors (17)

1005. H.J.RES.4
Proposing a balanced budget amendment to the Constitution of the United States.
Sponsor: Rep. Buchanan, Vern [R-FL-13] (Introduced 01/05/2011)
Cosponsors (2)

1006. H.J.RES.5
Proposing an amendment to the Constitution of the United States to control spending.
Sponsor: Rep. Hensarling, Jeb [R-TX-5] (Introduced 01/05/2011)
Cosponsors (4)

1007. H.J.RES.6
Proposing an amendment to the Constitution of the United States waiving the application of the first article of amendment to the political speech of corporations and other business organizations with respect

to the disbursement of funds in connection with public elections and granting Congress and the States the power to establish limits on contributions and expenditures in elections for public office.
Sponsor: Rep. Kaptur, Marcy [D-OH-9] (Introduced 01/05/2011)
Cosponsors (0)

1008. H.J.RES.7
Proposing an amendment to the Constitution of the United States waiving the application of the first article of amendment to the political speech of corporations and other business organizations with respect to the disbursement of funds in connection with public elections.
Sponsor: Rep. Kaptur, Marcy [D-OH-9] (Introduced 01/05/2011)
Cosponsors (0)

1009. H.J.RES.8
Proposing an amendment to the Constitution of the United States relating to limitations on the amounts of contributions and expenditures that may be made in connection with campaigns for election to public office.
Sponsor: Rep. Kaptur, Marcy [D-OH-9] (Introduced 01/05/2011)
Cosponsors (8)

1010. H.J.RES.10
Proposing a balanced budget amendment to the Constitution of the United States.
Sponsor: Rep. Cuellar, Henry [D-TX-28] (Introduced 01/06/2011)
Cosponsors (18)

1011. H.J.RES.11
Proposing an amendment to the Constitution of the United States to balance the Federal budget.
Sponsor: Rep. Broun, Paul C. [R-GA-10] (Introduced 01/07/2011)
Cosponsors (24)

1012. H.J.RES.13
Proposing an amendment to the Constitution of the United States giving Congress power to prohibit the physical desecration of the flag of the United States.
Sponsor: Rep. Emerson, Jo Ann [R-MO-8] (Introduced 01/07/2011)
Cosponsors (91)

1013. H.J.RES.14
Proposing an amendment to the Constitution to provide for a balanced budget for the United States Government and for greater accountability in the enactment of tax legislation.
Sponsor: Rep. Emerson, Jo Ann [R-MO-8] (Introduced 01/07/2011)
Cosponsors (0)

1014. H.J.RES.15
Proposing an amendment to the Constitution of the United States to authorize the line item veto.
Sponsor: Rep. Platts, Todd Russell [R-PA-19] (Introduced 01/07/2011)
Cosponsors (2)

1015. H.J.RES.16
Proposing an amendment to the Constitution of the United States to repeal the sixteenth article of amendment.
Sponsor: Rep. King, Steve [R-IA-5] (Introduced 01/07/2011)
Cosponsors (1)

1016. H.J.RES.17
Proposing an amendment to the Constitution of the United States to repeal the twenty-second article of amendment, thereby removing the limitation on the number of terms an individual may serve as President.
Sponsor: Rep. Serrano, Jose E. [D-NY-16] (Introduced 01/07/2011)
Cosponsors (0)

1017. H.J.RES.18
Proposing a balanced budget amendment to the Constitution of the United States.
Sponsor: Rep. Terry, Lee [R-NE-2] (Introduced 01/07/2011)
Cosponsors (0)

1018. H.J.RES.20
Proposing an amendment to the Constitution of the United States to limit the number of consecutive terms that a Member of Congress may serve.
Sponsor: Rep. Platts, Todd Russell [R-PA-19] (Introduced 01/18/2011)
Cosponsors (8)

1019. H.J.RES.22
Preserving Capitalism in America Amendment

Sponsor: Rep. Turner, Michael R. [R-OH-3] (Introduced 01/24/2011)
Cosponsors (0)

1020. H.J.RES.23 — Proposing an amendment to the Constitution of the United States requiring that the Federal budget be balanced.
Sponsor: Rep. Schweikert, David [R-AZ-5] (Introduced 02/08/2011)
Cosponsors (6)

1021. H.J.RES.24
Proposing an amendment to the Constitution of the United States [requiring concurrence of two-thirds of the Members of each house of Congress for final adoption of any legislation changing the internal revenue laws, unless such legislation is determined not to increase the internal revenue by more than a de minimus amount].
Sponsor: Rep. Neugebauer, Randy [R-TX-19] (Introduced 02/08/2011)
Cosponsors (5)

1022. H.J.RES.25 : Proposing an amendment to the Constitution of the United States regarding presidential election voting rights for residents of all United States territories and commonwealths.
Sponsor: Del. Christensen, Donna M. [D-VI-At Large] (Introduced 02/09/2011)
Cosponsors (2)

1023. H.J.RES.26
Proposing an amendment to the Constitution of the United States relating to Congressional succession.
Sponsor: Rep. Rohrabacher, Dana [R-CA-46] (Introduced 02/11/2011)
Cosponsors (0)

1024. H.J.RES.27
Proposing an amendment to the Constitution of the United States restoring religious freedom.
Sponsor: Rep. Stearns, Cliff [R-FL-6] (Introduced 02/14/2011)
Cosponsors (0)

1025. H.J.RES.28
Proposing an amendment to the Constitution of the United States regarding the right to vote.
Sponsor: Rep. Jackson, Jesse L., Jr. [D-IL-2] (Introduced 02/14/2011)
Cosponsors (51)

1026. H.J.RES.29

Proposing an amendment to the Constitution of the United States regarding the right of all citizens of the United States to a public education of equal high quality.

Sponsor: Rep. Jackson, Jesse L., Jr. [D-IL-2] (Introduced 02/14/2011)

Cosponsors (28)

1027. H.J.RES.30

Proposing an amendment to the Constitution of the United States regarding the right of citizens of the United States to health care of equal high quality.

Sponsor: Rep. Jackson, Jesse L., Jr. [D-IL-2] (Introduced 02/14/2011)

Cosponsors (28)

1028. H.J.RES.31

Proposing an amendment to the Constitution of the United States relating to equality of rights and reproductive rights.

Sponsor: Rep. Jackson, Jesse L., Jr. [D-IL-2] (Introduced 02/14/2011)

Cosponsors (29)

1029. H.J.RES.32

Proposing an amendment to the Constitution of the United States respecting the right to decent, safe, sanitary, and affordable housing.

Sponsor: Rep. Jackson, Jesse L., Jr. [D-IL-2] (Introduced 02/14/2011)

Cosponsors (28)

1030. H.J.RES.33

Proposing an amendment the Constitution of the United States respecting the right to a clean, safe, and sustainable environment.

Sponsor: Rep. Jackson, Jesse L., Jr. [D-IL-2] (Introduced 02/14/2011)

Cosponsors (28)

1031. H.J.RES.34

Proposing an amendment to the Constitution of the United States relative to taxing the people of the United States progressively.

Sponsor: Rep. Jackson, Jesse L., Jr. [D-IL-2] (Introduced 02/14/2011)

Cosponsors (28)

1032. H.J.RES.35

Proposing an amendment to the Constitution of the United States respecting the right to full employment and balanced growth.

Sponsor: Rep. Jackson, Jesse L., Jr. [D-IL-2] (Introduced 02/14/2011)
Cosponsors (28)

1033. H.J.RES.36
Proposing an amendment to the Constitution of the United States to abolish the Electoral College and provide for the direct election of the President and Vice President by the popular vote of all citizens of the United States regardless of place of residence.
Sponsor: Rep. Jackson, Jesse L., Jr. [D-IL-2] (Introduced 02/14/2011)
Cosponsors (29)

1034. H.J.RES.41
Proposing a balanced budget amendment to the Constitution of the United States.
Sponsor: Rep. DeFazio, Peter A. [D-OR-4] (Introduced 02/17/2011)
Cosponsors (1)

1035. H.J.RES.45
Proposing an amendment to the Constitution of the United States relating to marriage.
Sponsor: Rep. Broun, Paul C. [R-GA-10] (Introduced 03/03/2011)
Cosponsors (32)

1036. H.J.RES.46
Proposing an amendment to the Constitution of the United States to allow the several States to nullify a law or regulation of the United States.
Sponsor: Rep. Griffith, H. Morgan [R-VA-9] (Introduced 03/03/2011)
Cosponsors (1)
***1037. H.J.RES.47**: Removing the deadline for the ratification of the equal rights amendment.
Sponsor: Rep. Baldwin, Tammy [D-WI-2] (Introduced 03/08/2011)
Cosponsors (56)

1038. H.J.RES.50: Proposing an amendment to the Constitution of the United States relative to abolishing personal income, estate, and gift taxes and prohibiting the United States Government from engaging in business in competition with its citizens.
Sponsor: Rep. Paul, Ron [R-TX-14] (Introduced 03/15/2011)
Cosponsors (0)

1039. H.J.RES.51
Proposing an amendment to the Constitution of the United States to control Federal spending.
Sponsor: Rep. Akin, W. Todd [R-MO-2] (Introduced 03/30/2011)
Cosponsors (1)

1040. H.J.RES.52
Proposing an amendment to the Constitution of the United States requiring that the Federal budget be balanced.
Sponsor: Rep. Buchanan, Vern [R-FL-13] (Introduced 03/30/2011)
Cosponsors (2)

1041. H.J.RES.53
Proposing an amendment to the Constitution of the United States to limit the number of years Representatives and Senators may serve.
Sponsor: Rep. Price, Tom [R-GA-6] (Introduced 03/31/2011)
Cosponsors (2)

1042. H.J.RES.54
Proposing an amendment to the Constitution of the United States relative to balancing the budget.
Sponsor: Rep. Walsh, Joe [R-IL-8] (Introduced 04/06/2011)
Cosponsors (14)

1043. H.J.RES.56
Proposing an amendment to the Constitution of the United States relative to balancing the budget.
Sponsor: Rep. Walsh, Joe [R-IL-8] (Introduced 04/07/2011)
Cosponsors (61)

1044. H.J.RES.57
Proposing an amendment to the Constitution of the United States allowing the States to call a limited convention solely for the purposes of considering whether to propose a specific amendment to the Constitution.
Sponsor: Rep. Culberson, John Abney [R-TX-7] (Introduced 05/10/2011)
Cosponsors (1)

1045. H.J.RES.62
Proposing an amendment to the Constitution of the United States to

give States the right to repeal Federal laws and regulations when ratified by the Legislatures of two thirds of the several States.
Sponsor: Rep. Bishop, Rob [R-UT-1] (Introduced 05/12/2011)
Cosponsors (16)

1046. H.J.RES.63
Proposing an amendment to the Constitution of the United States to require a two-thirds vote of each House of Congress to increase the statutory limit on the public debt.
Sponsor: Rep. Neugebauer, Randy [R-TX-19] (Introduced 05/13/2011)
Cosponsors (0)

1047. H.J.RES.65
Proposing an amendment to the Constitution of the United States to prohibit candidates for election to Congress from accepting contributions from individuals who do not reside in the State or Congressional district the candidate seeks to represent.
Sponsor: Rep. Boren, Dan [D-OK-2] (Introduced 05/24/2011)
Cosponsors (0)

1048. H.J.RES.69
Proposing an amendment to the Constitution of the United States relative to equal rights for men and women.
Sponsor: Rep. Maloney, Carolyn B. [D-NY-14] (Introduced 06/22/2011)
Cosponsors (186)

1049. H.J.RES.71
Proposing an amendment to the Constitution of the United States limiting the number of terms that a Member of Congress may serve to 3 in the House of Representatives and 2 in the Senate.
Sponsor: Rep. Schweikert, David [R-AZ-5] (Introduced 07/07/2011)
Cosponsors (8)

1050. H.J.RES.72
Proposing an amendment to the Constitution of the United States giving Congress power to regulate campaign contributions for Federal elections.
Sponsor: Rep. Schrader, Kurt [D-OR-5] (Introduced 07/13/2011)
Cosponsors (6)

1051. H.J.RES.73
Proposing a spending limit amendment to the Constitution of the United States.
Sponsor: Rep. Amash, Justin [R-MI-3] (Introduced 07/21/2011)
Cosponsors (43)

1052. H.J.RES.75
Proposing an amendment to the Constitution of the United States relating to the use of foreign law as authority in Federal courts.
Sponsor: Rep. Culberson, John Abney [R-TX-7] (Introduced 08/05/2011)
Cosponsors (0)

1053. H.J.RES.76
Proposing an amendment to the Constitution of the United States regarding the effect of treaties, Executive orders, and agreements with other nations or groups of nations.
Sponsor: Rep. Culberson, John Abney [R-TX-7] (Introduced 08/05/2011)
Cosponsors (0)

1054. H.J.RES.78
Proposing an amendment to the Constitution of the United States to clarify the authority of Congress and the States to regulate the expenditure of funds for political activity by corporations.
Sponsor: Rep. Edwards, Donna F. [D-MD-4] (Introduced 09/12/2011)
Cosponsors (39)

1055. H.J.RES.81
Proposing a balanced budget amendment to the Constitution of the United States.
Sponsor: Rep. Amash, Justin [R-MI-3] (Introduced 10/14/2011)
Cosponsors (59)

1056. H.J.RES.82
Proposing an amendment to the Constitution of the United States authorizing regulation of any expenditure in connection with an election.
Sponsor: Rep. Deutch, Theodore E. [D-FL-19] (Introduced 10/14/2011)
Cosponsors (0)

1057. H.J.RES.84

Proposing an amendment to the Constitution of the United States prohibiting the United States government from increasing its debt except for a specific purpose by law adopted by three-fourths of the membership of each House of Congress.

Sponsor: Rep. McClintock, Tom [R-CA-4] (Introduced 11/04/2011)

Cosponsors (11)

1058. H.J.RES.86: Proposing an amendment to the Constitution of the United States relating to contributions and expenditures with respect to elections.

Sponsor: Rep. Sutton, Betty [D-OH-13] (Introduced 11/14/2011)

Cosponsors (15)

1059. H.J.RES.87 : Proposing a balanced budget amendment to the Constitution of the United States.

Sponsor: Rep. Carney, John C., Jr. [D-DE-At Large] (Introduced 11/15/2011)

Cosponsors (7)

1060. H.J.RES.88

Proposing an amendment to the Constitution of the United States to clarify the authority of Congress and the States to regulate corporations, limited liability companies or other corporate entities established by the laws of any state, the United States, or any foreign state.

Sponsor: Rep. McGovern, James P. [D-MA-3] (Introduced 11/15/2011)

Cosponsors (31)

1061. H.J.RES.89

Proposing a balanced budget amendment to the Constitution of the United States.

Sponsor: Rep. Castor, Kathy [D-FL-11] (Introduced 11/17/2011)

Cosponsors (0)

1062. H.J.RES.90

Proposing an amendment to the Constitution of the United States to expressly exclude for-profit corporations from the rights given to natural persons by the Constitution of the United States, prohibit corporate spending in all elections, and affirm the authority of Congress and the States to regulate corporations and to regulate and set limits on all election contributions and expenditures.

Sponsor: Rep. Deutch, Theodore E. [D-FL-19] (Introduced 11/18/2011)
Cosponsors (55)

1063. H.J.RES.92
Proposing an amendment to the Constitution of the United States relating to the authority of Congress and the States to regulate the disbursement of funds for political activity by for-profit corporations and other for-profit business organizations.
Sponsor: Rep. Ellison, Keith [D-MN-5] (Introduced 12/06/2011)
Cosponsors (6)

1064. H.J.RES.93
Proposing an amendment to the Constitution of the United States relating to limits on the number of terms a Member of Congress may serve.
Sponsor: Rep. Coffman, Mike [R-CO-6] (Introduced 12/15/2011)
Cosponsors (3)

1065. H.J.RES.96
Proposing an amendment to the Constitution of the United States to limit the number of terms that a Member of Congress may serve to 4 in the House of Representatives and 2 in the Senate.
Sponsor: Rep. Fitzpatrick, Michael G. [R-PA-8] (Introduced 12/20/2011)
Cosponsors (1)

1066. H.J.RES.97
Proposing an amendment to the Constitution of the United States relating to contributions and expenditures with respect to Federal elections.
Sponsor: Rep. Yarmuth, John A. [D-KY-3] (Introduced 12/20/2011)
Cosponsors (5)

1067. H.J.RES.99
Proposing an amendment to the Constitution of the United States to require that an increase in the Federal debt requires approval from a majority of the legislatures of the several States.
Sponsor: Rep. Schweikert, David [R-AZ-5] (Introduced 01/17/2012)
Cosponsors (7)

1068. H.J.RES.100 : Proposing an amendment to the Constitution of the United States regarding the use of public funds to pay for campaigns for election to Federal office.
Sponsor: Rep. Kucinich, Dennis J. [D-OH-10] (Introduced 01/18/2012)

Cosponsors (5)

1069. H.J.RES.101
Proposing an amendment to the Constitution of the United States providing for Representatives to be chosen every four years, and limiting the number of times Senators and Representatives may be elected.
Sponsor: Rep. Ribble, Reid J. [R-WI-8] (Introduced 02/06/2012)
Cosponsors (4)

1070. H.J.RES.102
Proposing a balanced budget amendment to the Constitution of the United States.
Sponsor: Rep. Chabot, Steve [R-OH-1] (Introduced 2/14/2012)
Cosponsors (7)

1071. H.J.RES.105
Proposing an amendment to the Constitution of the United States limiting the number of times Senators and Representatives may be elected.
Sponsor: Rep. Ribble, Reid J. [R-WI-8] (Introduced 02/29/2012)
Cosponsors (2)

1072. H.J.RES.106
Proposing an amendment to the Constitution of the United States to protect the rights of crime victims.
Sponsor: Rep. Franks, Trent [R-AZ-2] (Introduced 03/26/2012)
Cosponsors (18)

1073. H.J.RES.107
Proposing an amendment to the Constitution of the United States relating to parental rights.
Sponsor: Rep. Franks, Trent [R-AZ-2] (Introduced 03/29/2012)
Cosponsors (21)

1074. H.J.RES.110: Proposing an amendment to the Constitution of the United States relating to parental rights.
Sponsor: Rep. Franks, Trent [R-AZ-2] (Introduced 06/05/2012)
Cosponsors (85)

1075. H.J.RES.111: Proposing an amendment to the Constitution of the United States relating to the authority of Congress and the States to regulate contributions and expenditures in political campaigns and to

enact public financing systems for such campaigns.
Sponsor: Rep. Schiff, Adam B. [D-CA-29] (Introduced 06/18/2012)
Cosponsors (17)

1076 H.J.RES.114
Proposing an amendment to the Constitution of the United States relative to construing provisions of law as having been enacted pursuant to the power of Congress to lay and collect taxes.
Sponsor: Rep. Quayle, Benjamin [R-AZ-3] (Introduced 06/29/2012)
Cosponsors (0)

1077 H.J.RES.116
Proposing an amendment to the Constitution of the United States which requires (except during time of war and subject to suspension by Congress) that the total amount of money expended by the United States during any fiscal year not exceed the amount of certain revenue received by the United States during such fiscal year and not exceed 20 percent of the gross domestic product of the United States during the previous calendar year.
Sponsor: Rep. Roby, Martha [R-AL-2] (Introduced 07/25/2012)
Cosponsors (0)

1078. H.J.RES.121
Proposing an amendment to the Constitution of the United States to increase by 29 votes the number of electoral votes awarded to the candidate for President who receives the largest percentage of the popular vote.
Sponsor: Rep. Israel, Steve [D-NY-2] (Introduced 10/23/2012)
Cosponsors (0)

Senate

1079. S.J.RES.1
A joint resolution proposing an amendment to the Constitution of the United States relative to limiting the number of terms that a Member of Congress may serve.
Sponsor: Sen. Vitter, David [R-LA] (Introduced 01/25/2011)
Cosponsors (2)

1080. S.J.RES.2
A joint resolution proposing an amendment to the Constitution of the United States relating to United States citizenship.
Sponsor: Sen. Vitter, David [R-LA] (Introduced 01/25/2011)
Cosponsors (1)

1081. S.J.RES.3
A joint resolution proposing an amendment to the Constitution of the United States relative to balancing the budget.
Sponsor: Sen. Hatch, Orrin G. [R-UT] (Introduced 01/26/2011)
Cosponsors (32)

1082. S.J.RES.4
A joint resolution proposing an amendment to the Constitution of the United States which requires (except during time of war and subject to suspension by Congress) that the total amount of money expended by the United States during any fiscal year not exceed the amount of certain revenue received by the United States during such fiscal year and not to exce ed 20 per cent of the gross national product of the United States during the previous calendar year.
Sponsor: Sen. Shelby, Richard C. [R-AL] (Introduced 02/01/2011)
Cosponsors (5)

1083. S.J.RES.5
A joint resolution proposing an amendment to the Constitution of the United States requiring that the Federal budget be balanced.
Sponsor: Sen. Lee, Mike [R-UT] (Introduced 02/03/2011)
Cosponsors (19)

1084. S.J.RES.10
Joint resolution proposing a balanced budget amendment to the Constitution of the United States.

Sponsor: Sen. Hatch, Orrin G. [R-UT] (Introduced 03/31/2011)
Cosponsors (47)

1085. S.J.RES.11
A joint resolution proposing an amendment to the Constitution of the United States relative to limiting the number of terms that a Member of Congress may serve to 3 in the House of Representatives and 2 in the Senate.
Sponsor: Sen. DeMint, Jim [R-SC] (Introduced 04/14/2011)
Cosponsors (10)

1086. S.J.RES.12
A joint resolution proposing an amendment to the Constitution of the United States to give States the right to repeal Federal laws and regulations when ratified by the legislatures of two-thirds of the several States.
Sponsor: Sen. Enzi, Michael B. [R-WY] (Introduced 05/12/2011)
Cosponsors (4)

1087. S.J.RES.19
A joint resolution proposing an amendment to the Constitution of the United States authorizing Congress to prohibit the physical desecration of the flag of the United States.
Sponsor: Sen. Hatch, Orrin G. [R-UT] (Introduced 06/14/2011)
Cosponsors (37)

1088. S.J.RES.21
A joint resolution proposing an amendment to the Constitution of the United States relative to equal rights for men and women.
Sponsor: Sen. Menendez, Robert [D-NJ] (Introduced 06/22/2011)
Cosponsors (15)

1089. S.J.RES.23
A joint resolution proposing an amendment to the Constitution of the United States relative to balancing the budget.
Sponsor: Sen. McConnell, Mitch [R-KY] (Introduced 06/29/2011)
Cosponsors (46)

1090. S.J.RES.24
Joint resolution proposing a balanced budget amendment to the Constitution of the United States.
Sponsor: Sen. Udall, Mark [D-CO] (Introduced 08/02/2011
Cosponsors (5)

1091. S.J.RES.29
A joint resolution proposing an amendment to the Constitution of the United States relating to contributions and expenditures intended to affect elections.
Sponsor: Sen. Udall, Tom [D-NM] (Introduced 11/01/2011)
Cosponsors (25)

1092. S.J.RES.35
A joint resolution proposing an amendment to the Constitution of the United States relative to authorizing regulation of contributions to candidates for State public office and Federal office by corporations, entities organized and operated for profit, and labor organizations, and expenditures by such entities and labor organizations in support of, or opposition to such candidates.
Sponsor: Sen. Baucus, Max [D-MT] (Introduced 01/24/2012)
Cosponsors (1)
***1093. S.J.RES.39:** A joint resolution removing the deadline for the ratification of the equal rights amendment.
Sponsor: Sen. Cardin, Benjamin L. [D-MD] (Introduced 03/22/2012)
Cosponsors (17)

1094. S.J.RES.42
A joint resolution proposing an amendment to the Constitution of the United States relative to parental rights.
Sponsor: Sen. DeMint, Jim [R-SC] (Introduced 06/05/2012)
Cosponsors (12)

113th Congress (2013-2014)

House

1095. H.J. RES.1
Proposing a balanced budget amendment to the Constitution of the United States.
Sponsor: Rep. Goodlatte, Bob [R-VA-6] (Introduced 01/03/2013)
Cosponsors (91)

1096. H.J.RES.2
Proposing a balanced budget amendment to the Constitution of the United States.
Sponsor: Rep. Goodlatte, Bob [R-VA-6] (Introduced 01/03/2013)
Cosponsors (142)

1097. H.J.RES.4
Proposing a balanced budget amendment to the Constitution of the United States.
Sponsor: Rep. Barrow, John [D-GA-12] (Introduced 01/03/2013)
Cosponsors (10)

1098. H.J.RES.5
Proposing an amendment to the Constitution of the United States relative to balancing the budget.
Sponsor: Rep. Buchanan, Vern [R-FL-13] (Introduced 01/03/2013)
Cosponsors (2)

1099. H.J.RES.6
Proposing a balanced budget amendment to the Constitution of the United States.
Sponsor: Rep. Buchanan, Vern [R-FL-13] (Introduced 01/03/2013)
Cosponsors (0)

1100. H.J.RES.7
Proposing an amendment to the Constitution of the United States regarding presidential election voting rights for residents of all United States territories and commonwealths.

Sponsor: Del. Christensen, Donna M. [D-VI-At Large] (Introduced 01/03/2013)

Cosponsors (1)

1101. H.J.RES.8

Proposing an amendment to the Constitution of the United States to limit the number of terms that a Member of Congress may serve to 4 in the House of Representatives and 2 in the Senate.

Sponsor: Rep. Fitzpatrick, Michael G. [R-PA-8] (Introduced 01/03/2013)

Cosponsors (0)

1102. H.J.RES.9

Proposing an amendment to the Constitution of the United States prohibiting the United States government from increasing its debt except for a specific purpose by law adopted by three-fourths of the membership of each House of Congress.

Sponsor: Rep. McClintock, Tom [R-CA-4] (Introduced 01/03/2013)

Cosponsors (0)

1103. H.J.RES.10

Proposing an amendment to the Constitution of the United States requiring that the Federal budget be balanced and that an increase in the Federal debt requires approval from a majority of the legislatures of the several States.

Sponsor: Rep. Schweikert, David [R-AZ-5] (Introduced 01/03/2013)

Cosponsors (0)

1104. H.J RES.11: Proposing a balanced budget amendment to the Constitution of the United States.

Sponsor: Rep. Terry, Lee [R-NE-2] (Introduced 01/03/2013)

Cosponsors (9)

1105. H.J.RES.12

Proposing an amendment to the Constitution of the United States relating to limitations on the amounts of contributions and expenditures that may be made in connection with campaigns for election to public office.

Sponsor: Rep. Kaptur, Marcy [D-OH-9] (Introduced 01/04/2013)

Cosponsors (1)

1106. H.J.RES.13

Proposing an amendment to the Constitution of the United States waiv-

ing the application of the first article of amendment to the political speech of corporations and other business organizations with respect to the disbursement of funds in connection with public elections.
Sponsor: Rep. Kaptur, Marcy [D-OH-9] (Introduced 01/04/2013)
Cosponsors (0)

1107. H.J.RES.14
Proposing an amendment to the Constitution of the United States waiving the application of the first article of amendment to the political speech of corporations and other business organizations with respect to the disbursement of funds in connection with public elections and granting Congress and the States the power to establish limits on contributions and expenditures in elections for public office.
Sponsor: Rep. Kaptur, Marcy [D-OH-9] (Introduced 01/04/2013)
Cosponsors (0)

1108. H.J.RES.15
Proposing an amendment to the Constitution of the United States to repeal the twenty-second article of amendment, thereby removing the limitation on the number of terms an individual may serve as President.
Sponsor: Rep. Serrano, Jose E. [D-NY-15] (Introduced 01/04/2013)
Cosponsors (0)

1109. H.J.RES.16
Proposing an amendment to the Constitution of the United States to repeal the sixteenth article of amendment.
Sponsor: Rep. King, Steve [R-IA-4] (Introduced 01/04/2013)
Cosponsors (3)

1110. H.J.RES.17
Proposing an amendment to the Constitution of the United States which requires (except during time of war and subject to suspension by Congress) that the total amount of money expended by the United States during any fiscal year not exceed the amount of certain revenue received by the United States during such fiscal year and not exceed 20 percent of the gross domestic product of the United States during the previous calendar year.
Sponsor: Rep. Roby, Martha [R-AL-2] (Introduced 01/15/2013)
Cosponsors (0)

1111. H.J.RES.18

Proposing an amendment to the Constitution to provide for a balanced budget for the United States Government and for greater accountability in the enactment of tax legislation.

Sponsor: Rep. Emerson, Jo Ann [R-MO-8] (Introduced 01/18/2013)

Cosponsors (0)

1112. H.J.RES.19

Proposing an amendment to the Constitution of the United States giving Congress power to prohibit the physical desecration of the flag of the United States.

Sponsor: Rep. Emerson, Jo Ann [R-MO-8] (Introduced 01/18/2013)

Cosponsors (4)

1113. H.J.RES.20

Proposing an amendment to the Constitution of the United States relating to contributions and expenditures with respect to elections.

Sponsor: Rep. McGovern, James P. [D-MA-2] (Introduced 01/22/2013)

Cosponsors (37)

1114. H.J.RES.21

Proposing an amendment to the Constitution of the United States to clarify the authority of Congress and the States to regulate corporations, limited liability companies or other corporate entities established by the laws of any State, the United States, or any foreign state.

Sponsor: Rep. McGovern, James P. [D-MA-2] (Introduced 01/22/2013)

Cosponsors (36)

1115. H.J.RES.22

Proposing an amendment to the Constitution of the United States to limit the number of consecutive terms that a Member of Congress may serve.

Sponsor: Rep. Harris, Andy [R-MD-1] (Introduced 01/22/2013)

Cosponsors (0)

1116. H.J.RES.23: Proposing an amendment to the Constitution of the United States to limit the number of consecutive terms that a Member of Congress may serve.

Sponsor: Rep. Duffy, Sean P. [R-WI-7] (Introduced 01/25/2013)

Cosponsors (0)

1117. H.J.RES.24
Proposing a balanced budget amendment to the Constitution of the United States.
Sponsor: Rep. Amash, Justin [R-MI-3] (Introduced 02/06/2013)
Cosponsors (38)

1118. H.J.RES.25
Proposing an amendment to the Constitution of the United States to clarify the authority of Congress and the States to regulate the expenditure of funds for political activity by corporations.
Sponsor: Rep. Edwards, Donna F. [D-MD-4] (Introduced 02/06/2013)
Cosponsors (53)

1119. H.J.RES.26: Proposing an amendment to the Constitution of the United States to limit the number of consecutive terms that a Member of Congress may serve.
Sponsor: Rep. Barr, Andy [R-KY-6] (Introduced 02/12/2013)
Cosponsors (8)

1120. H.J.RES.27
Proposing an amendment to the Constitution of the United States prohibiting the Federal Government from using the power of taxation to compel someone to engage in commercial activity.
Sponsor: Rep. Bentivolio, Kerry L. [R-MI-11] (Introduced 02/13/2013)
Cosponsors (3)

1121. H.J.RES.28
Proposing an amendment to the Constitution of the United States to limit the power of Congress to impose a tax on a failure to purchase goods or services.
Sponsor: Rep. Palazzo, Steven M. [R-MS-4] (Introduced 02/13/2013)
Cosponsors (37)

1122. H.J.RES.29
Proposing an amendment to the Constitution of the United States providing that the rights extended by the Constitution are the rights of natural persons only.
Sponsor: Rep. Nolan, Richard M. [D-MN-8] (Introduced 02/14/2013)
Cosponsors (3)

1123. H.J.RES.30

Proposing an amendment to the Constitution of the United States to limit the number of years Representatives and Senators may serve.

Sponsor: Rep. Price, Tom [R-GA-6] (Introduced 02/14/2013)

Cosponsors (0)

1124. H.J.RES.31

Proposing an amendment to the Constitution of the United States relating to the authority of Congress and the States to regulate contributions and expenditures in political campaigns and to enact public financing systems for such campaigns.

Sponsor: Rep. Schiff, Adam B. [D-CA-28] (Introduced 02/14/2013)

Cosponsors (20)

1125. H.J.RES.32

Proposing an amendment to the Constitution of the United States giving Congress power to regulate campaign contributions for Federal elections.

Sponsor: Rep. Schrader, Kurt [D-OR-5] (Introduced 02/26/2013)

Cosponsors (0)

1126. H.J.RES.33

Proposing an amendment to the Constitution of the United States to prohibit a law increasing the compensation for the services of the Senators and Representatives from taking effect until an election of Representatives has intervened, and to permit a law otherwise varying such compensation to take effect upon enactment.

Sponsor: Rep. Barrow, John [D-GA-12] (Introduced 03/06/2013)

Cosponsors (3)

1127. H.J.RES.34

Proposing an amendment to the Constitution of the United States to restore the rights of the American people that were taken away by the Supreme Court's decision in the Citizens United case and related decisions, to protect the integrity of our elections, and to limit the corrosive influence of money in our democratic process.

Sponsor: Rep. Deutch, Theodore E. [D-FL-21] (Introduced 03/12/2013)

Cosponsors (75)

1128. H.J.RES.35

Proposing an amendment to the Constitution of the United States to

balance the Federal budget.
Sponsor: Rep. Broun, Paul C. [R-GA-10] (Introduced 03/14/2013)
Cosponsors (18)

1129. H.J.RES.36: Proposing a balanced budget amendment to the Constitution requiring that each agency and department's funding is justified.
Sponsor: Rep. Perry, Scott [R-PA-4] (Introduced 03/14/2013)
Cosponsors (8)

1130. H.J.RES.37
Proposing an amendment to the Constitution of the United States limiting the number of times Senators and Representatives may be elected.
Sponsor: Rep. Ribble, Reid J. [R-WI-8] (Introduced 03/18/2013)
Cosponsors (0)

1131. H.J.RES.38
Proposing a balanced budget amendment to the Constitution of the United States.
Sponsor: Rep. Walorski, Jackie [R-IN-2] (Introduced 04/12/2013)
Cosponsors (0)

1132. H.J.RES.39
Proposing an amendment to the Constitution of the United States [proposing two-thirds majority of Congress to raise revenue].
Sponsor: Rep. Neugebauer, Randy [R-TX-19] (Introduced 04/15/2013)
Cosponsors (0)

1133. H.J.RES.40
Proposing an amendment to the Constitution of the United States to protect the rights of crime victims
Sponsor: Rep. Franks, Trent [R-AZ-8] (Introduced 04/23/2013)
Cosponsors (19)

1134. H.J.RES.41
Proposing an amendment to the Constitution of the United States relative to limiting the number of terms that a Member of Congress may serve.
Sponsor: Rep. Salmon, Matt [R-AZ-5] (Introduced 04/23/2013)
Cosponsors (17)

1135. H.J.RES.42
Proposing an amendment to the Constitution of the United States to clarify that the Constitution neither prohibits voluntary prayer nor requires prayer in schools.
Sponsor: Rep. Rahall, Nick J., II [D-WV-3] (Introduced 04/26/2013)
Cosponsors (0)

***1136. H.J.RES.43**
Removing the deadline for the ratification of the equal rights amendment.
Sponsor: Rep. Andrews, Robert E. [D-NJ-1] (Introduced 05/09/2013)
Cosponsors (105)

1137. H.J.RES.44
Proposing an amendment to the Constitution of the United States regarding the right to vote.
Sponsor: Rep. Pocan, Mark [D-WI-2] (Introduced 05/14/2013)
Cosponsors (26)

1138. H.J.RES.45
Proposing an amendment to the Constitution of the United States granting Congress the authority to enact laws limiting the number of terms that Representatives and Senators may serve.
Sponsor: Rep. Bridenstine, Jim [R-OK-1] (Introduced 05/14/2013)
Cosponsors (1)

1139. H.J.RES.47
Proposing an amendment to the Constitution of the United States giving Congress power to prohibit the physical desecration of the flag of the United States.
Sponsor: Rep. Bachus, Spencer [R-AL-6] (Introduced 05/22/2013)
Cosponsors (32)

1140. H.J.RES.48
Proposing an amendment to the Constitution of the United States to limit the number of consecutive terms that a Member of Congress may serve.
Sponsor: Rep. Marino, Tom [R-PA-10] (Introduced 05/22/2013)
Cosponsors (0)

1141. H.J.RES.49
Proposing a balanced budget amendment to the Constitution of the United States.
Sponsor: Rep. Smith, Jason [R-MO-8] (Introduced 06/14/2013)
Cosponsors (0)

1142. H.J.RES.50
Proposing an amendment to the Constitution of the United States relating to parental rights.
Sponsor: Rep. Meadows, Mark [R-NC-11] (Introduced 06/18/2013)
Cosponsors (80)

1143. H.J.RES.51
Marriage Protection Amendment
Sponsor: Rep. Huelskamp, Tim [R-KS-1] (Introduced 06/28/2013)
Cosponsors (58)

1144. H.J.RES.52
Proposing an amendment to the Constitution of the United States allowing the States to call a limited convention solely for the purposes of considering whether to propose a specific amendment to the Constitution.
Sponsor: Rep. Culberson, John Abney [R-TX-7] (Introduced 07/24/2013)
Cosponsors (3)

1145. H.J.RES.53
Proposing an amendment to the Constitution of the United States regarding the effect of treaties, Executive orders, and agreements with other nations or groups of nations.
Sponsor: Rep. Culberson, John Abney [R-TX-7] (Introduced 07/24/2013)
Cosponsors (5)

1146. H.J.RES.54
Proposing an amendment to the Constitution of the United States relating to the use of foreign law as authority in Federal courts.
Sponsor: Rep. Culberson, John Abney [R-TX-7] (Introduced 07/24/2013)
Cosponsors (4)

1147. H.J.RES.55

Proposing an amendment to the Constitution of the United States relating to the equal application to the Senators and Representatives of the laws that apply to all citizens of the United States.

Sponsor: Rep. DeSantis, Ron [R-FL-6] (Introduced 08/01/2013)

Cosponsors (10)

1148. H.J.RES.56

Proposing an amendment to the Constitution of the United States relative to equal rights for men and women.

Sponsor: Rep. Maloney, Carolyn B. [D-NY-12] (Introduced 08/01/2013)

Cosponsors (176)

1149. H.J.RES.57

Proposing an amendment to the Constitution of the United States to require a two-thirds vote of each House of Congress to increase the statutory limit on the public debt.

Sponsor: Rep. Neugebauer, Randy [R-TX-19] (Introduced 08/01/2013)

Cosponsors (0)

1150. H.J.RES.97

Proposing an amendment to the Constitution of the United States relative to applying laws equally to the citizens of the United States and the Federal Government.

Sponsor: Rep. Jenkins, Lynn [R-KS-2] (Introduced 10/22/2013)

Cosponsors (0)

1151. H.J.RES.98

Proposing an amendment to the Constitution of the United States relative to applying laws equally to the citizens of the United States and the Federal Government.

Sponsor: Rep. Duncan, Jeff [R-SC-3] (Introduced 10/23/2013)

Cosponsors (8)

1152. H.J.RES.101

Proposing an amendment to the Constitution of the United States to limit the number of consecutive terms that a Member of Congress may serve.

Sponsor: Rep. Palazzo, Steven M. [R-MS-4] (Introduced 10/30/2013)

Cosponsors (1)

1153. H.J.RES.104
Proposing an amendment to the Constitution of the United States to repeal the sixteenth article of amendment.
Sponsor: Rep. Bridenstine, Jim [R-OK-1] (Introduced 11/15/2013)
Cosponsors (12)

1154. H.J.RES.107
Proposing an amendment to the Constitution of the United States relating to contributions and expenditures with respect to Federal elections.
Sponsor: Rep. Yarmuth, John A. [D-KY-3] (Introduced 01/16/2014)
Cosponsors (3)

1155. H.J.RES.108
Proposing an amendment to the Constitution of the United States to limit the number of terms that a Member of Congress may serve.
Sponsor: Rep. Mulvaney, Mick [R-SC-5] (Introduced 02/04/2014)
Cosponsors (9)

***1156. H.J.RES.113**
Removing the deadline for the ratification of the equal rights amendment.
Sponsor: Rep. Speier, Jackie [D-CA-14] (Introduced 03/27/2014)
Cosponsors (147)

1157 H.J.RES.114: Proposing an amendment to the Constitution of the United States concerning the election of the Members of the House of Representatives.
Sponsor: Rep. Larson, John B. [D-CT-1] (Introduced 04/10/2014)
Cosponsors (0)

1158. H.J.RES.115
Proposing an amendment to the Constitution of the United States to give States the right to repeal Federal laws and regulations when ratified by the legislatures of two-thirds of the several States.
Sponsor: Rep. Bishop, Rob [R-UT-1] (Introduced 05/21/2014)
Cosponsors (20)

1159. H.J.RES.119
Proposing an amendment to the Constitution of the United States relating to contributions and expenditures intended to affect elections.
Sponsor: Rep. Deutch, Theodore E. [D-FL-21] (Introduced 07/14/2014)
Cosponsors (129)

1160. H.J.RES.121

Proposing an amendment to the Constitution of the United States relating to the authority of Congress and the States to regulate political campaign contributions and expenditures, including independent expenditures.

Sponsor: Rep. Carney, John C., Jr. [D-DE-At Large] (Introduced 07/29/2014)

Cosponsors (0)

1161. H.J.RES.122

Proposing an amendment to the Constitution of the United States to end the practice of including more than one subject in a single law by requiring that each law enacted by Congress be limited to only one subject and that the subject be clearly and descriptively expressed in the title of the law.

Sponsor: Rep. Marino, Tom [R-PA-10] (Introduced 07/31/2014)

Cosponsors (0)

1162 H.J.RES.126

Proposing an amendment to the Constitution of the United States to control entitlement spending.

Sponsor: Rep. Crawford, Eric A. "Rick" [R-AR-1] (Introduced 09/18/2014)

Cosponsors (20)

Senate

1163. S.J.RES.1

A joint resolution proposing an amendment to the Constitution of the United States requiring that the Federal budget be balanced.

Sponsor: Sen. Lee, Mike [R-UT] (Introduced 01/22/2013)

Cosponsors (0)

1164. S.J.RES.2

A joint resolution proposing an amendment to the Constitution of the United States relative to limiting the number of terms that a Member of Congress may serve.

Sponsor: Sen. Vitter, David [R-LA] (Introduced 01/23/2013)

Cosponsors (11)

1165. S.J.RES.3

A joint resolution proposing an amendment to the Constitution of the United States relative to limiting the number of terms that a Member of Congress may serve to 3 in the House of Representatives and 2 in the Senate.

Sponsor: Sen. Paul, Rand [R-KY] (Introduced 01/23/2013)

Cosponsors (1)

1166. S.J.RES.4

A joint resolution proposing an amendment to the Constitution of the United States relating to United States citizenship.

Sponsor: Sen. Vitter, David [R-LA] (Introduced 01/23/2013)

Cosponsors (0)

1167. S.J.RES.5

A joint resolution proposing an amendment to the Constitution of the United States relative to authorizing regulation of contributions to candidates for State public office and Federal office by corporations, entities organized and operated for profit, and labor organization, and expenditures by such entities and labor organizations in support of, or opposition to such candidates.

Sponsor: Sen. Baucus, Max [D-MT] (Introduced 01/28/2013)

Cosponsors (1)

1168. S.J.RES.6

A joint resolution proposing an amendment to the Constitution of the

United States which requires (except during time of war and subject to suspension by Congress) that the total amount of money expended by the United States during any fiscal year not exceed the amount of certain revenue received by the United States during such fiscal year and not exceed 20 percent of the gross domestic product of the United States during the previous calendar year.
Sponsor: Sen. Shelby, Richard C. [R-AL] (Introduced 01/29/2013)
Cosponsors (1)

1169. S.J.RES.7
A joint resolution proposing an amendment to the Constitution of the United States relative to balancing the budget.
Sponsor: Sen. Cornyn, John [R-TX] (Introduced 02/13/2013)
Cosponsors (44)

1170. S.J.RES.10
A joint resolution proposing an amendment to the Constitution of the United States relative to equal rights for men and women.
Sponsor: Sen. Menendez, Robert [D-NJ] (Introduced 03/05/2013)
Cosponsors (17)

1171. S.J.RES.11
A joint resolution proposing an amendment to the Constitution of the United States to restore the rights of the American people that were taken away by the Supreme Court's decision in the Citizens United case and related decisions, to protect the integrity of our elections, and to limit the corrosive influence of money in our democratic process.
Sponsor: Sen. Sanders, Bernard [I-VT] (Introduced 03/13/2013)
Cosponsors (1)

***1172. S.J.RES.15**
A joint resolution removing the deadline for the ratification of the equal rights amendment.
Sponsor: Sen. Cardin, Benjamin L. [D-MD] (Introduced 05/09/2013)
Cosponsors (35)

1173. S.J.RES.16
A joint resolution proposing an amendment to the Constitution of the United States to limit the power of Congress to impose a tax on a failure to purchase goods or services.
Sponsor: Sen. Rubio, Marco [R-FL] (Introduced 06/06/2013)
Cosponsors (8)

1174. S.J.RES.17
A joint resolution proposing an amendment to the Constitution of the United States authorizing Congress to prohibit the physical desecration of the flag of the United States.
Sponsor: Sen. Hatch, Orrin G. [R-UT] (Introduced 06/13/2013)
Cosponsors (23)

1175. S.J.RES.18
A joint resolution proposing an amendment to the Constitution of the United States to clarify the authority of Congress and the States to regulate corporations, limited liability companies or other corporate entities established by the laws of any State, the United States, or any foreign state.
Sponsor: Sen. Tester, Jon [D-MT] (Introduced 06/18/2013)
Cosponsors (5)

1176. S.J.RES.19
A joint resolution proposing an amendment to the Constitution of the United States relating to contributions and expenditures intended to affect elections.
Sponsor: Sen. Udall, Tom [D-NM] (Introduced 06/18/2013)
Cosponsors (48)

1177. S.J.RES.20
A joint resolution proposing a balanced budget amendment to the Constitution of the United States.
Sponsor: Sen. Udall, Mark [D-CO] (Introduced 07/11/2013)
Cosponsors (6

1178. S.J.RES.25
A joint resolution proposing an amendment to the Constitution of the United States relative to applying laws equally to the citizens of the United States and the Federal Government.
Sponsor: Sen. Paul, Rand [R-KY] (Introduced 10/11/2013)
Cosponsors (0)

1179. S.J.RES.34
A joint resolution proposing an amendment to the Constitution of the United States to give States the right to repeal Federal laws and regulations when ratified by the legislatures of two-thirds of the several States.
Sponsor: Sen. Enzi, Michael B. [R-WY] (Introduced 03/13/2014)
Cosponsors (2)

1180. S.J.RES.37 : A joint resolution proposing an amendment to the Constitution of the United States relating to parental rights.
Sponsor: Sen. Graham, Lindsey [R-SC] (Introduced 06/04/2014)
Cosponsors (5)

114th Congress (2015-2016)

House

11181. H.J.RES.1
Proposing a balanced budget amendment to the Constitution of the United States. **S**
Sponsor: Rep. Goodlatte, Bob [R-VA-6] (Introduced 01/06/2015)
Cosponsors (89)

1182. H.J.RES.2
Proposing a balanced budget amendment to the Constitution of the United States.
Sponsor: Rep. Goodlatte, Bob [R-VA-6] (Introduced 01/06/2015)
Cosponsors (110)

1183. H.J.RES.4
Proposing an amendment to the Constitution of the United States relative to balancing the budget.
Sponsor: Rep. Buchanan, Vern [R-FL-16] (Introduced 01/06/2015)
Cosponsors (1)

1184. H.J.RES.5
Proposing an amendment to the Constitution of the United States regarding the effect of treaties, Executive orders, and agreements with other nations or groups of nations.
Sponsor: Rep. Culberson, John Abney [R-TX-7] (Introduced 01/06/2015)
Cosponsors (0

1185. H.J.RES.6
Proposing an amendment to the Constitution of the United States to limit the number of terms that a Member of Congress may serve to 4 in the House of Representatives and 2 in the Senate.
Sponsor: Rep. Fitzpatrick, Michael G. [R-PA-8] (Introduced 01/06/2015)
Cosponsors (0)

1186. H.J.RES.7
Proposing a balanced budget amendment to the Constitution of the United States.
Sponsor: Rep. Lance, Leonard [R-NJ-7] (Introduced 01/06/2015)
Cosponsors (2)

1187. H.J.RES.8
Proposing an amendment to the Constitution of the United States requiring that the Federal budget be balanced and that an increase in the Federal debt requires approval from a majority of the legislatures of the several States.
Sponsor: Rep. Schweikert, David [R-AZ-6] (Introduced 01/06/2015)
Cosponsors (1)

1188. H.J.RES.9
Proposing an amendment to the Constitution of the United States giving Congress power to prohibit the physical desecration of the flag of the United States.
Sponsor: Rep. Womack, Steve [R-AR-3] (Introduced 01/06/2015)
Cosponsors (43)

1189. H.J.RES.11
Proposing an amendment to the Constitution of the United States to limit the number of consecutive terms that a Member of Congress may serve.
Sponsor: Rep. Barr, Andy [R-KY-6] (Introduced 01/09/2015)
Cosponsors (25)

1190. H.J.RES.12: Proposing a balanced budget amendment to the Constitution of the United States.
Sponsor: Rep. Byrne, Bradley [R-AL-1] (Introduced 01/09/2015)
Cosponsors (3)

1191. H.J.RES.13
Proposing an amendment to the Constitution of the United States to limit the number of terms that a Member of Congress may serve.
Sponsor: Rep. Mulvaney, Mick [R-SC-5] (Introduced 01/09/2015)
Cosponsors (12)

1192. H.J.RES.14
Proposing an amendment to the Constitution of the United States to

limit the number of terms that a Member of Congress may serve.
Sponsor: Rep. Salmon, Matt [R-AZ-5] (Introduced 01/09/2015)
Cosponsors (17)

1193. H.J.RES.15
Proposing an amendment to the Constitution of the United States granting Congress the authority to enact laws limiting the number of terms that Representatives and Senators may serve.
Sponsor: Rep. Bridenstine, Jim [R-OK-1] (Introduced 01/12/2015)
Cosponsors (0)

1194 H.J.RES.16
Proposing an amendment to the Constitution of the United States to repeal the sixteenth article of amendment.
Sponsor: Rep. King, Steve [R-IA-4] (Introduced 01/12/2015)
Cosponsors (1)

1195. H.J.RES.17
Proposing an amendment to the Constitution of the United States relative to balancing the budget.
Sponsor: Rep. Buchanan, Vern [R-FL-16] (Introduced 01/12/2015)
Cosponsors (1)

1196. H.J.RES.18
Proposing an amendment to the Constitution of the United States prohibiting the United States Government from increasing its debt except for a specific purpose by law adopted by three-fourths of the membership of each House of Congress.
Sponsor: Rep. McClintock, Tom [R-CA-4] (Introduced 01/12/2015)
Cosponsors (0)

1197 H.J.RES.19
Proposing an amendment to the Constitution of the United States to limit the number of consecutive terms that a Member of Congress may serve.
Sponsor: Rep. Palazzo, Steven M. [R-MS-4] (Introduced 01/12/2015)
Cosponsors (2)

1198. H.J.RES.20: Proposing an amendment to the Constitution of the United States to limit Congress' power to impose a tax on a failure to purchase goods or services.

Sponsor: Rep. Palazzo, Steven M. [R-MS-4] (Introduced 01/12/2015)
Cosponsors (3)

1199. H.J.RES.21
Proposing an amendment to the Constitution of the United States to limit the number of consecutive terms that a Member of Congress may serve.
Sponsor: Rep. Duffy, Sean P. [R-WI-7] (Introduced 01/14/2015)
Cosponsors (0)

1200. H.J.RES.22
Proposing an amendment to the Constitution of the United States relating to contributions and expenditures intended to affect elections.
Sponsor: Rep. Deutch, Theodore E. [D-FL-21] (Introduced 01/20/2015)
Cosponsors (162)

1201. H.J.RES.23
Proposing an amendment to the Constitution of the United States to clarify the authority of Congress and the States to regulate corporations, limited liability companies or other corporate entities established by the laws of any State, the United States, or any foreign state.
Sponsor: Rep. McGovern, James P. [D-MA-2] (Introduced 01/21/2015)
Cosponsors (22)

1202. H.J.RES.24
Proposing an amendment to the Constitution of the United States relating to the authority of Congress and the States to regulate political campaign contributions and expenditures, including independent expenditures.
Sponsor: Rep. Carney, John C., Jr. [D-DE-At Large] (Introduced 01/21/2015)
Cosponsors (0)

1203. H.J.RES.25
Proposing an amendment to the Constitution of the United States regarding the right to vote.
Sponsor: Rep. Pocan, Mark [D-WI-2] (Introduced 01/21/2015)
Cosponsors (40)

1204. H.J.RES.26
Proposing an amendment to the Constitution of the United States to

limit the number of years Representatives and Senators may serve.
Sponsor: Rep. Price, Tom [R-GA-6] (Introduced 01/26/2015)
Cosponsors (0)

1205. H.J.RES.28
Proposing a balanced budget amendment to the Constitution requiring that each agency and department's funding is justified.
Sponsor: Rep. Perry, Scott [R-PA-4] (Introduced 02/03/2015)
Cosponsors (0)

1206. H.J.RES.31: Proposing an amendment to the Constitution of the United States regarding the permissible sources of funding for elections for public office and State ballot measures.
Sponsor: Rep. McNerney, Jerry [D-CA-9] (Introduced 02/11/2015)
Cosponsors (0)

1207. H.J.RES.32
Marriage Protection Amendment
Sponsor: Rep. Huelskamp, Tim [R-KS-1] (Introduced 02/12/2015)
Cosponsors (37)

1208. H.J.RES.34
Proposing an amendment to the Constitution of the United States allowing the States to call a limited convention solely for the purposes of considering whether to propose a specific amendment to the Constitution.
Sponsor: Rep. Culberson, John Abney [R-TX-7] (Introduced 02/13/2015)
Cosponsors (1)

1209. H.J.RES.36
Proposing an amendment to the Constitution of the United States to clarify the authority of Congress and the States to regulate the expenditure of funds for political activity by corporations.
Sponsor: Rep. Edwards, Donna F. [D-MD-4] (Introduced 02/26/2015)
Cosponsors (15)

1210. H.J.RES.38
Proposing an amendment to the Constitution of the United States waiving the application of the first article of amendment to the political speech of corporations and other business organizations with respect

to the disbursement of funds in connection with public elections and granting Congress and the States the power to establish limits on contributions and expenditures in elections for public office.
Sponsor: Rep. Kaptur, Marcy [D-OH-9] (Introduced 03/17/2015)
Cosponsors (0)

1211 H.J.RES.39
Proposing an amendment to the Constitution of the United States to limit the number of consecutive terms that a Member of Congress may serve.
Sponsor: Rep. Marino, Tom [R-PA-10] (Introduced 03/26/2015)
Cosponsors (0)

1212. H.J.RES.40
Proposing an amendment to the Constitution of the United States to end the practice of including more than one subject in a single law by requiring that each law enacted by Congress be limited to only one subject and that the subject be clearly and descriptively expressed in the title of the law.
Sponsor: Rep. Marino, Tom [R-PA-10] (Introduced 03/26/2015)
Cosponsors (0)

1213. H.J.RES.41
Proposing a balanced budget amendment to the Constitution of the United States.
Sponsor: Rep. Ratcliffe, John [R-TX-4] (Introduced 03/26/2015)
Cosponsors (1)

1214. H.J.RES.45
Proposing an amendment to the Constitution of the United States to protect the rights of crime victims.
Sponsor: Rep. Franks, Trent [R-AZ-8] (Introduced 04/16/2015)
Cosponsors (6)

1215. H.J.RES.46
Proposing an amendment to the Constitution of the United States giving Congress power to regulate campaign contributions for Federal elections.
Sponsor: Rep. Schrader, Kurt [D-OR-5] (Introduced 04/21/2015)
Cosponsors (0)

1216. H.J.RES.48
Proposing an amendment to the Constitution of the United States providing that the rights extended by the Constitution are the rights of natural persons only.
Sponsor: Rep. Nolan, Richard M. [D-MN-8] (Introduced 04/28/2015)
Cosponsors (23)

1217. H.J.RES.49
Proposing an amendment to the Constitution of the United States to limit the number of terms that a Member of Congress may serve.
Sponsor: Rep. DeSantis, Ron [R-FL-6] (Introduced 05/05/2015)
Cosponsors (5)

***1218. H.J.RES.51**
Removing the deadline for the ratification of the equal rights amendment.
Sponsor: Rep. Speier, Jackie [D-CA-14] (Introduced 05/13/2015)
Cosponsors (164)

1219. H.J.RES.52: Proposing an amendment to the Constitution of the United States relative to equal rights for men and women.
Sponsor: Rep. Maloney, Carolyn B. [D-NY-12] (Introduced 05/14/2015)
Cosponsors (194)

1220. H.J.RES.53
Proposing an amendment to the Constitution of the United States relating to contributions and expenditures with respect to Federal elections.
Sponsor: Rep. Yarmuth, John A. [D-KY-3] (Introduced 05/14/2015)
Cosponsors (1)

1221 H.J.RES.54
Proposing a balanced budget amendment to the Constitution of the United States.
Sponsor: Rep. Amash, Justin [R-MI-3] (Introduced 05/18/2015)
Cosponsors (5)

1222. H.J.RES.55
Proposing a balanced budget amendment to the Constitution of the United States.
Sponsor: Rep. Brat, Dave [R-VA-7] (Introduced 05/20/2015)
Cosponsors (65)

1223. H.J.RES.58

Proposing an amendment to the Constitution of the United States relating to the authority of Congress and the States to regulate contributions and expenditures in political campaigns and to enact public financing systems for such campaigns.

Sponsor: Rep. Schiff, Adam B. [D-CA-28] (Introduced 06/24/2015)

Cosponsors (16)

1224. H.J.RES.69

Proposing a balanced budget amendment to the Constitution of the United States.

Sponsor: Rep. Carney, John C., Jr. [D-DE-At Large] (Introduced 10/08/2015)

Cosponsors (0)

1225. H.J.RES.79

Proposing a balanced budget amendment to the Constitution of the United States.

Sponsor: Rep. Hardy, Cresent [R-NV-4] (Introduced 12/16/2015)

Cosponsors (0)

1226. H.J.RES.80

Fair Districts Amendment [restricting gerrymandering of congressional districts].

Sponsor: Rep. Grayson, Alan [D-FL-9] (Introduced 01/11/2016)

Cosponsors (0)

1227. H.J.RES.81

Proposing a balanced budget amendment to the Constitution of the United States.

Sponsor: Rep. Stivers, Steve [R-OH-15] (Introduced 01/13/2016)

Cosponsors (1)

1228. H.J.RES.83

Proposing a balanced budget amendment to the Constitution of the United States.

Sponsor: Rep. Ashford, Brad [D-NE-2] (Introduced 03/02/2016)

Cosponsors (6)

1229. H.J.RES.85

Proposing an amendment to the Constitution of the United States requiring that the Federal budget be balanced.

Sponsor: Rep. Loudermilk, Barry [R-GA-11] (Introduced 03/03/2016)
Cosponsors (20)

1230. H.J.RES.86
Proposing an amendment to the Constitution of the United States to provide for balanced budgets for the Government.
Sponsor: Rep. DeFazio, Peter A. [D-OR-4] (Introduced 04/14/2016)
Cosponsors (0)

1231. H.J.RES.89
Proposing an amendment to the Constitution of the United States relating to the equal application to the Senators and Representatives of the laws that apply to all citizens of the United States.
Sponsor: Rep. DeSantis, Ron [R-FL-6] (Introduced 04/20/2016)
Cosponsors (7)

1232. H.J.RES.91
Proposing an amendment to the Constitution of the United States relating to parental rights.
Sponsor: Rep. Franks, Trent [R-AZ-8] (Introduced 04/26/2016)
Cosponsors (10)

1233. H.J.RES.92
Proposing an amendment to the Constitution of the United States to give States the right to repeal Federal laws and regulations when ratified by the legislatures of two-thirds of the several States.
Sponsor: Rep. Bishop, Rob [R-UT-1] (Introduced 05/10/2016)
Cosponsors (1)

1234. H.J.RES.93
Proposing a balanced budget amendment to the Constitution of the United States.
Sponsor: Rep. Gohmert, Louie [R-TX-1] (Introduced 05/10/2016)
Cosponsors (1)

1235. H.J.RES.96
Proposing an amendment to the Constitution of the United States to prohibit the President from making recess appointments.
Sponsor: Rep. Collins, Chris [R-NY-27] (Introduced 07/05/2016)
Cosponsors (5)

1236. H.J.RES.97
Proposing an amendment to the Constitution of the United States to make a quality education a civil right.
Sponsor: Rep. Honda, Michael M. [D-CA-17] (Introduced 07/14/2016)
Cosponsors (5)

1237. H.J.Res.100
Proposing an amendment to the Constitution of the United States to give States the authority to repeal a Federal rule or regulation when ratified by the legislatures of two-thirds of the several States.
Sponsor: Rep. Bishop, Rob [R-UT-1] (Introduced 09/28/2016)
Cosponsors (3)

1238. H.J.RES.101
Proposing an amendment to the Constitution of the United States which requires (except during time of war and subject to suspension by Congress) that the total amount of money expended by the United States during any fiscal year not exceed the amount of certain revenue received by the United States during such fiscal year and not exceed 20 percent of the gross domestic product of the United States during the previous calendar year.
Sponsor: Rep. Roby, Martha [R-AL-2] (Introduced 09/28/2016)
Cosponsors (0)

1239. H.J.RES.102
Every Vote Counts Amendment
Sponsor: Rep. Green, Gene [D-TX-29] (Introduced 11/17/2016)
Cosponsors (19)

1240. H.J.RES.103
Proposing an amendment to the Constitution of the United States to abolish the electoral college and to provide for the direct popular election of the President and Vice President of the United States.
Sponsor: Rep. Rangel, Charles B. [D-NY-13] (Introduced 11/17/2016)
Cosponsors (2)

1241. H.J.RES.104
Proposing an amendment to the Constitution of the United States to abolish the electoral college and to provide for the direct election of the President and Vice President of the United States.
Sponsor: Rep. Cohen, Steve [D-TN-9] (Introduced 12/01/2016)
Cosponsors (1)

1242. H.J.RES.105

Proposing an amendment to the Constitution of the United States to treat Puerto Rico as if it were a State for purposes of the election of the President and Vice President.

Sponsor: Rep. Grayson, Alan [D-FL-9] (Introduced 12/02/2016)

Cosponsors (0)

Senate

1243. S.J.RES.1
A joint resolution proposing an amendment to the Constitution of the United States relative to limiting the number of terms that a Member of Congress may serve.
Sponsor: Sen. Vitter, David [R-LA] (Introduced 01/06/2015)
Cosponsors (14)

1244. S.J.RES.2
A joint resolution proposing an amendment to the Constitution of the United States requiring that the Federal budget be balanced.
Sponsor: Sen. Lee, Mike [R-UT] (Introduced 01/06/2015)
Cosponsors (2)

1245. S.J.RES.4 :A joint resolution proposing an amendment to the Constitution of the United States to restore the rights of the American people that were taken away by the Supreme Court's decision in the Citizens United case and related decisions, to protect the integrity of our elections, and to limit the corrosive influence of money in our democratic process.
Sponsor: Sen. Sanders, Bernard [I-VT] (Introduced 01/21/2015)
Cosponsors (0)

1246. S.J.RES.5
A joint resolution proposing an amendment to the Constitution of the United States relating to contributions and expenditures intended to affect elections.
Sponsor: Sen. Udall, Tom [D-NM] (Introduced 01/21/2015)
Cosponsors (42)

1247. S.J.RES.6
A joint resolution proposing an amendment to the Constitution of the United States relative to balancing the budget.
Sponsor: Sen. Hatch, Orrin G. [R-UT] (Introduced 02/04/2015)
Cosponsors (53)

1248. S.J.RES.7
A joint resolution proposing an amendment to the Constitution of the United States to clarify the authority of Congress and the States to regulate corporations, limited liability companies, and other corporate enti-

ties established by the laws of any State, the United States, or any foreign state.
Sponsor: Sen. Tester, Jon [D-MT] (Introduced 02/04/2015)
Cosponsors (1)

1249. S.J.RES.9
A joint resolution proposing an amendment to the Constitution of the United States which requires (except during time of war and subject to suspension by Congress) that the total amount of money expended by the United States during any fiscal year not exceed the amount of certain revenue received by the United States during such fiscal year and not exceed 20 percent of the gross domestic product of the United States during the previous calendar year.
Sponsor: Sen. Shelby, Richard C. [R-AL] (Introduced 02/09/2015)
Cosponsors (0)

1250. S.J.RES.12
A joint resolution proposing an amendment to the Constitution of the United States relative to marriage.
Sponsor: Sen. Cruz, Ted [R-TX] (Introduced 04/23/2015)
Cosponsors (0)

1251. S.J.RES.13
A joint resolution proposing an amendment to the Constitution of the United States relative to applying laws equally to the citizens of the United States and the Federal Government.
Sponsor: Sen. Paul, Rand [R-KY] (Introduced 04/23/2015)
Cosponsors (0)

*1252. S.J.RES.15
A joint resolution removing the deadline for the ratification of the equal rights amendment.
Sponsor: Sen. Cardin, Benjamin L. [D-MD] (Introduced 05/07/2015)
Cosponsors (30)

1253. S.J.RES.16
A joint resolution proposing an amendment to the Constitution of the United States relative to equal rights for men and women.
Sponsor: Sen. Menendez, Robert [D-NJ] (Introduced 05/07/2015)
Cosponsors (10)

1254. S.J.RES.17
A joint resolution proposing an amendment to the Constitution of the United States to give States the right to repeal Federal laws and regulations when ratified by the legislatures of two-thirds of the several States.
Sponsor: Sen. Enzi, Michael B. [R-WY] (Introduced 06/25/2015)
Cosponsors (0)

1255. S.J.RES.18
A joint resolution proposing a balanced budget amendment to the Constitution of the United States.
Sponsor: Sen. Donnelly, Joe [D-IN] (Introduced 07/09/2015)
Cosponsors (3)

1256. S.J.RES.21
A joint resolution proposing an amendment to the Constitution of the United States authorizing the Congress to prohibit the physical desecration of the flag of the United States.
Sponsor: Sen. Vitter, David [R-LA] (Introduced 07/30/2015)
Cosponsors (9)

1257. S.J.RES.36
A joint resolution proposing an amendment to the Constitution of the United States relating to parental rights.
Sponsor: Sen. Graham, Lindsey [R-SC] (Introduced 06/29/2016)
Cosponsors (5)

1258. S.J.RES.41
A joint resolution proposing an amendment to the Constitution of the United States to abolish the electoral college and to provide for the direct popular election of the President and Vice President of the United States.
Sponsor: Sen. Boxer, Barbara [D-CA] (Introduced 11/15/2016)
Cosponsors (3)

115th Congress (2017-2018)

House

1259. H.J.RES.1
Proposing a balanced budget amendment to the Constitution of the United States.
Sponsor: Rep. Goodlatte, Bob [R-VA-6] (Introduced 01/03/2017)
Cosponsors (38)

1260. H.J.RES.2
Proposing a balanced budget amendment to the Constitution of the United States.
Sponsor: Rep. Goodlatte, Bob [R-VA-6] (Introduced 01/03/2017)
Cosponsors (65)

1261. H.J.RES.4
Proposing an amendment to the Constitution of the United States granting Congress the authority to enact laws limiting the number of terms that Representatives and Senators may serve.
Sponsor: Rep. Bridenstine, Jim [R-OK-1] (Introduced 01/03/2017)
Cosponsors (1)

1262. H.J.RES.5
Proposing an amendment to the Constitution of the United States relative to balancing the budget.
Sponsor: Rep. Buchanan, Vern [R-FL-16] (Introduced 01/03/2017)
Cosponsors (0)

1263. H.J.RES.6
Proposing an amendment to the Constitution of the United States to limit the number of terms that a Member of Congress may serve.
Sponsor: Rep. DeSantis, Ron [R-FL-6] (Introduced 01/03/2017)
Cosponsors (43)

1264. H.J.RES.7
Proposing an amendment to the Constitution of the United States to limit the number of years an individual may serve as a Member of Con-

gress.
Sponsor: Rep. Fitzpatrick, Brian K. [R-PA-8] (Introduced 01/03/2017)
Cosponsors (3)

1265, H.J.RES.8
Proposing an amendment to the Constitution of the United States to provide for balanced budgets for the Government.
Sponsor: Rep. Fitzpatrick, Brian K. [R-PA-8] (Introduced 01/03/2017)
Cosponsors (1)

1266. H.J.RES.9
Proposing an amendment to the Constitution of the United States to prohibit Members of Congress from receiving compensation during a fiscal year unless both Houses of Congress have agreed to a concurrent resolution on the budget for that fiscal year prior to the beginning of that fiscal year.
Sponsor: Rep. Fitzpatrick, Brian K. [R-PA-8] (Introduced 01/03/2017)
Cosponsors (3)

1267 H.J.RES.12
Proposing an amendment to the Constitution of the United States prohibiting the United States Government from increasing its debt except for a specific purpose by law adopted by three-fourths of the membership of each House of Congress.
Sponsor: Rep. McClintock, Tom [R-CA-4] (Introduced 01/03/2017)
Cosponsors (4)

1268. H.J.RES.13
Proposing an amendment to the Constitution of the United States to limit the number of terms a Representative or Senator may serve.
Sponsor: Rep. O'Rourke, Beto [D-TX-16] (Introduced 01/03/2017)
Cosponsors (1)

1269. H.J.RES.14
Proposing a balanced budget amendment to the Constitution of the United States.
Sponsor: Rep. Byrne, Bradley [R-AL-1] (Introduced 01/04/2017)
Cosponsors (1)

1270. H.J.RES.15
Proposing a balanced budget amendment to the Constitution of the

United States.
Sponsor: Rep. Amash, Justin [R-MI-3] (Introduced 01/04/2017)
Cosponsors (2)

1271. H.J.RES.17
Proposing an amendment to the Constitution of the United States to limit the number of consecutive terms that a Member of Congress may serve.
Sponsor: Rep. Palazzo, Steven M. [R-MS-4] (Introduced 01/04/2017)
Cosponsors (8)

1272. H.J.RES.18
Proposing a balanced budget amendment to the Constitution requiring that each agency and department's funding is justified.
Sponsor: Rep. Perry, Scott [R-PA-4] (Introduced 01/04/2017)
Cosponsors (0)

1273. H.J.RES.19
Proposing an amendment to the Constitution of the United States to abolish the electoral college and to provide for the direct election of the President and Vice President of the United States.
Sponsor: Rep. Cohen, Steve [D-TN-9] (Introduced 01/05/2017)
Cosponsors (5)

1274. H.J.RES.20
Proposing an amendment to the Constitution of the United States to limit the number of consecutive terms that a Member of Congress may serve.
Sponsor: Rep. Duffy, Sean P. [R-WI-7] (Introduced 01/05/2017)
Cosponsors (0)

1275. H.J.RES.21
Proposing an amendment to the Constitution of the United States to limit Congress' power to impose a tax on a failure to purchase goods or services.
Sponsor: Rep. Palazzo, Steven M. [R-MS-4] (Introduced 01/06/2017)
Cosponsors (2)

1276. H.J.RES.23
Proposing an amendment to the Constitution of the United States to limit the number of terms that a Member of Congress may serve to four

in the House of Representatives and two in the Senate.
Sponsor: Rep. Hollingsworth, Trey [R-IN-9] (Introduced 01/09/2017)
Cosponsors (0)

1277. H.J.RES.24
Proposing an amendment to the Constitution of the United States to limit the number of years an individual may serve as a Member of Congress.
Sponsor: Rep. Marino, Tom [R-PA-10] (Introduced 01/09/2017)
Cosponsors (1)

1278. H.J.RES.25
Proposing an amendment to the Constitution of the United States to end the practice of including more than one subject in a single law by requiring that each law enacted by Congress be limited to only one subject and that the subject be clearly and descriptively expressed in the title of the law.
Sponsor: Rep. Marino, Tom [R-PA-10] (Introduced 01/09/2017)
Cosponsors (1)

1279. H.J.RES.28
Proposing an amendment to the Constitution of the United States to protect the voting rights of the citizens of the United States.
Sponsor: Rep. Engel, Eliot L. [D-NY-16] (Introduced 01/13/2017)
Cosponsors (2)

1280. H.J.RES.29
Proposing an amendment to the Constitution of the United States requiring that the Federal budget be balanced.
Sponsor: Rep. Loudermilk, Barry [R-GA-11] (Introduced 01/13/2017)
Cosponsors (14)

1281. H.J.RES.30
Proposing an amendment to the Constitution of the United States to provide that Representatives shall be apportioned among the several States according to their respective numbers, counting the number of persons in each State who are citizens of the United States.
Sponsor: Rep. King, Steve [R-IA-4] (Introduced 01/23/2017)
Cosponsors (0)

1282. H.J.RES.31

Proposing an amendment to the Constitution of the United States relating to contributions and expenditures intended to affect elections.
Sponsor: Rep. Deutch, Theodore E. [D-FL-22] (Introduced 01/24/2017)
Cosponsors (140)

1283. H.J.RES.32

Proposing an amendment to the Constitution of the United States to give States the authority to repeal Federal rules and regulations when the repeal is agreed to by the legislatures of two-thirds of the several States.
Sponsor: Rep. Bishop, Rob [R-UT-1] (Introduced 01/24/2017)
Cosponsors (3)

1284. H.J.RES.33

Proposing an amendment to the Constitution of the United States relative to equal rights for men and women.
Sponsor: Rep. Maloney, Carolyn B. [D-NY-12] (Introduced 01/24/2017)
Cosponsors (169)

1285. H.J.RES.48

Proposing an amendment to the Constitution of the United States providing that the rights extended by the Constitution are the rights of natural persons only.
Sponsor: Rep. Nolan, Richard M. [D-MN-8] (Introduced 01/30/2017)
Cosponsors (65)

1286. H.J.RES.50

Proposing an amendment to the Constitution of the United States to limit the number of terms a Representative or Senator may serve.
Sponsor: Rep. Labrador, Raul R. [R-ID-1] (Introduced 01/31/2017)
Cosponsors (13)

***1287. H.J.RES.53**

Removing the deadline for the ratification of the equal rights amendment.
Sponsor: Rep. Speier, Jackie [D-CA-14] (Introduced 01/31/2017)
Cosponsors (167)

1288. H.J.RES.61

Proposing an amendment to the Constitution of the United States giving Congress power to prohibit the physical desecration of the flag of the United States.

Sponsor: Rep. Womack, Steve [R-AR-3] (Introduced 02/02/2017)
Cosponsors (31)

1289. H.J.RES.64
— Proposing an amendment to the Constitution of the United States giving Congress power to regulate campaign contributions for Federal elections.
Sponsor: Rep. Schrader, Kurt [D-OR-5] (Introduced 02/06/2017)
Cosponsors (0)

1290. H.J.RES.65
Every Vote Counts Amendment
Sponsor: Rep. Green, Gene [D-TX-29] (Introduced 02/07/2017)
Cosponsors (25)

1291. H.J.RES.74
Proposing an amendment to the Constitution of the United States regarding the right to vote.
Sponsor: Rep. Pocan, Mark [D-WI-2] (Introduced 02/15/2017)
Cosponsors (37)

1292. H.J.RES.81
Proposing an amendment to the Constitution of the United States regarding health care.
Sponsor: Rep. McCollum, Betty [D-MN-4] (Introduced 02/16/2017)
Cosponsors (0)

1293. H.J.RES.85
Proposing an amendment to the Constitution of the United States limiting the number of terms Senators and Representatives may serve.
Sponsor: Rep. Gallagher, Mike [R-WI-8] (Introduced 03/01/2017)
Cosponsors (6)

1294. H.J.RES.88
Proposing an amendment to the Constitution of the United States to clarify the authority of Congress and the States to regulate corporations, limited liability companies or other corporate entities established by the laws of any State, the United States, or any foreign state.
Sponsor: Rep. McGovern, James P. [D-MA-2] (Introduced 03/10/2017)
Cosponsors (16)

1295. H.J.RES.90
Proposing an amendment to the Constitution of the United States to clarify the authority of Congress and the States to regulate the expenditure of funds for political activity by corporations.
Sponsor: Rep. Shea-Porter, Carol [D-NH-1] (Introduced 03/16/2017)
Cosponsors (7)

1296. H.J.RES.91
Proposing an amendment to the Constitution of the United States regarding Presidential election voting rights for residents of all United States territories and commonwealths.
Sponsor: Del. Plaskett, Stacey E. [D-VI-At Large] (Introduced 03/23/2017)
Cosponsors (1)

1297. H.J.RES.93 Proposing an amendment to the Constitution of the United States to protect the rights of crime victims.
Sponsor: Rep. Franks, Trent [R-AZ-8] (Introduced 04/03/2017)
Cosponsors (2)

1298. H.J.RES.94
Proposing an amendment to the Constitution of the United States to repeal the sixteenth article of amendment.
Sponsor: Rep. King, Steve [R-IA-4] (Introduced 04/05/2017)
Cosponsors (1)

1299. H.J.RES.98
Proposing a balanced budget amendment to the Constitution of the United States.
Sponsor: Rep. Ratcliffe, John [R-TX-4] (Introduced 04/08/2017)
Cosponsors (1)

1300. H.J.RES.101
Proposing an amendment to the Constitution of the United States to limit the number of terms an individual may serve as a Member of Congress.
Sponsor: Rep. Arrington, Jodey C. [R-TX-19] (Introduced 05/18/2017)
Cosponsors (4)

1301. H.J.RES.106
Proposing an amendment to the Constitution of the United States to

provide that Representatives shall be apportioned among the several States according to their respective numbers, counting the number of persons in each State who are citizens of the United States.
Sponsor: Rep. Davidson, Warren [R-OH-8] (Introduced 06/22/2017)
Cosponsors (3)

1302. H.J.RES.107
Proposing a balanced budget amendment to the Constitution of the United States.
Sponsor: Rep. Murphy, Stephanie N. [D-FL-7] (Introduced 06/29/2017)
Cosponsors (13)

1303. H.J.RES.109
Proposing an amendment to the Constitution of the United States to provide for balanced budgets for the Government.
Sponsor: Rep. DeFazio, Peter A. [D-OR-4] (Introduced 07/19/2017)
Cosponsors (0)

1304. H.J.RES.110
Proposing a balanced budget amendment to the Constitution of the United States.
Sponsor: Rep. Stivers, Steve [R-OH-15] (Introduced 07/19/2017)
Cosponsors (1)

1305. H.J.RES.113
Proposing an amendment to the Constitution of the United States relating to the authority of Congress and the States to regulate contributions and expenditures in political campaigns and to enact public financing systems for such campaigns.
Sponsor: Rep. Schiff, Adam B. [D-CA-28] (Introduced 07/20/2017)
Cosponsors (19)

1306. H.J.RES.114
Proposing an amendment to the Constitution of the United States which requires (except during time of war and subject to suspension by Congress) that the total amount of money expended by the United States during any fiscal year not exceed the amount of certain revenue received by the United States during such fiscal year and not exceed 20 percent of the gross domestic product of the United States during the previous calendar year.
Sponsor: Rep. Roby, Martha [R-AL-2] (Introduced 07/27/2017)
Cosponsors (0)

1307. H.J.RES.115
Proposing an amendment to the Constitution of the United States to clarify the presidential pardoning power.
Sponsor: Rep. Green, Al [D-TX-9] (Introduced 07/27/2017)
Cosponsors (3)

1308. H.J.RES.116
Proposing an amendment to the Constitution of the United States prohibiting Congress and the States from abridging the right of citizens to affordable, quality health care.
Sponsor: Rep. McEachin, A. Donald [D-VA-4] (Introduced 07/28/2017)
Cosponsors (12)

1309. H.J.RES.119
Proposing a balanced budget amendment to the Constitution of the United States.
Sponsor: Rep. Brat, Dave [R-VA-7] (Introduced 10/23/2017)
Cosponsors (15)

1310. H.J.RES.120
Proposing an amendment to the Constitution of the United States limiting the pardon power of the President.
Sponsor: Rep. Cohen, Steve [D-TN-9] (Introduced 10/31/2017)
Cosponsors (11)

1311. H.J.RES.121
Proposing an amendment to the Constitution of the United States relating to parental rights.
Sponsor: Rep. Hultgren, Randy [R-IL-14] (Introduced 11/16/2017)
Cosponsors (20)

1312. H.J.RES.126
Proposing an amendment to the Constitution of the United States relating to contributions and expenditures with respect to Federal elections.
Sponsor: Rep. Yarmuth, John A. [D-KY-3] (Introduced 01/19/2018)
Cosponsors (4)

1313. H.J.RES.134
Proposing an amendment to the Constitution of the United States to limit the number of terms an individual may serve as a Member of Congress.

Sponsor: Rep. Arrington, Jodey C. [R-TX-19] (Introduced 05/10/2018)
Cosponsors (10)

1314. H.J.RES.136
Proposing an amendment to the Constitution of the United States waiving the application of the first article of amendment to the political speech of corporations and other business organizations with respect to the disbursement of funds in connection with public elections and granting Congress and the States the power to establish limits on contributions and expenditures in elections for public office.
Sponsor: Rep. Kaptur, Marcy [D-OH-9] (Introduced 06/27/2018)
Cosponsors (2)

1315. H.J.RES.137
Proposing an amendment to the Constitution of the United States authorizing the territories of the United States to cast electoral votes in presidential elections.
Sponsor: Del. Bordallo, Madeleine Z. [D-GU-At Large] (Introduced 07/26/2018)
Cosponsors (0

1316. H.J.RES.138
Proposing an amendment to the Constitution of the United States extending the right to vote to citizens sixteen years of age or older.
Sponsor: Rep. Meng, Grace [D-NY-6] (Introduced 08/03/2018)
Cosponsors (0)

1317. H.J.RES.141
Proposing an amendment to the Constitution of the United States regarding the permissible sources of funding for elections for public office and State ballot measures.
Sponsor: Rep. McNerney, Jerry [D-CA-9] (Introduced 09/26/2018)
Cosponsors (1)

1318. H.J.RES.144
Proposing an amendment to the Constitution of the United States respecting the right to clean air, pure water, and the sustainable preservation of the ecological integrity, and aesthetic, scenic, and historical values of the natural environment.
Sponsor: Rep. McEachin, A. Donald [D-VA-4] (Introduced 12/11/2018)
Cosponsors (2)

1319. H.J.RES.146
Proposing an amendment to the Constitution of the United States to prohibit Members of Congress from receiving compensation for any period during which a Government shutdown is in effect.
Sponsor: Rep. Norman, Ralph [R-SC-5] (Introduced 12/21/2018)
Cosponsors (6)

Senate

1320. S.J.RES.2

A joint resolution proposing an amendment to the Constitution of the United States relative to limiting the number of terms that a Member of Congress may serve.

Sponsor: Sen. Cruz, Ted [R-TX] (Introduced 01/03/2017)

Cosponsors (14)

1321. S.J.RES.3

A joint resolution proposing an amendment to the Constitution of the United States which requires (except during time of war and subject to suspension by Congress) that the total amount of money expended by the United States during any fiscal year not exceed the amount of certain revenue received by the United States during such fiscal year and not exceed 20 percent of the gross domestic product of the United States during the previous calendar year.

Sponsor: Sen. Shelby, Richard C. [R-AL] (Introduced 01/04/2017)

Cosponsors (0)

***1322. S.J.RES.5**

A joint resolution removing the deadline for the ratification of the equal rights amendment.

Sponsor: Sen. Cardin, Benjamin L. [D-MD] (Introduced 01/17/2017)

Cosponsors (36)

1323. S.J.RES.6

A joint resolution proposing an amendment to the Constitution of the United States relative to equal rights for men and women.

Sponsor: Sen. Menendez, Robert [D-NJ] (Introduced 01/20/2017)

Cosponsors (15)

1324. S.J.RES.7

A joint resolution proposing an amendment to the Constitution of the United States requiring that the Federal budget be balanced.

Sponsor: Sen. Lee, Mike [R-UT] (Introduced 01/24/2017)

Cosponsors (1)

1325. S.J.RES.8

A joint resolution proposing an amendment to the Constitution of the United States relating to contributions and expenditures intended to affect elections.

Sponsor: Sen. Udall, Tom [D-NM] (Introduced 01/24/2017)
Cosponsors (42)

1326. S.J.RES.20
A joint resolution proposing an amendment to the Constitution of the United States to clarify the authority of Congress and the States to regulate corporations, limited liability companies, and other corporate entities established by the laws of any State, the United States, or any foreign state.
Sponsor: Sen. Tester, Jon [D-MT] (Introduced 02/03/2017)
Cosponsors (1)

1327. S.J.RES.24
A joint resolution proposing an amendment to the Constitution of the United States relative to balancing the budget.
Sponsor: Sen. Hatch, Orrin G. [R-UT] (Introduced 02/27/2017)
Cosponsors (50)

1328. S.J.RES.39
A joint resolution proposing a balanced budget amendment to the Constitution of the United States.
Sponsor: Sen. Donnelly, Joe [D-IN] (Introduced 03/30/2017)
Cosponsors (4)

1329. S.J.RES.46
A joint resolution proposing an amendment to the Constitution of the United States authorizing the Congress to prohibit the physical desecration of the flag of the United States.
Sponsor: Sen. Daines, Steve [R-MT] (Introduced 06/14/2017)
Cosponsors (13)

1330. S.J.RES.48
A joint resolution proposing an amendment to the Constitution of the United States relating to parental rights.
Sponsor: Sen. Graham, Lindsey [R-SC] (Introduced 08/01/2017)
Cosponsors (5)

1331. S.J.RES.51
A joint resolution proposing an amendment to the Constitution of the United States relative to limiting the number of terms that a Member of Congress may serve.

Sponsor: Sen. Cassidy, Bill [R-LA] (Introduced 12/21/2017)

Cosponsors (0)

116th Congress (2019-2020)

House

1332. H.J.RES.2
Proposing an amendment to the Constitution of the United States relating to contributions and expenditures intended to affect elections.
Sponsor: Rep. Deutch, Theodore E. [D-FL-22] (Introduced 01/03/2019)
Cosponsors (221)

1333 H.J.RES.4
Proposing an amendment to the Constitution of the United States to limit the number of terms an individual may serve as a Member of Congress.
Sponsor: Rep. Arrington, Jodey C. [R-TX-19] (Introduced 01/03/2019)
Cosponsors (12)

1334. H.J.RES.5
Proposing an amendment to the Constitution of the United States relative to balancing the budget.
Sponsor: Rep. Buchanan, Vern [R-FL-16] (Introduced 01/03/2019)
Cosponsors (1)

1335. H.J.RES.6
Proposing a balanced budget amendment to the Constitution of the United States.
Sponsor: Rep. Byrne, Bradley [R-AL-1] (Introduced 01/03/2019)
Cosponsors (5)

1336. H.J.RES.7
Proposing an amendment to the Constitution of the United States to abolish the electoral college and to provide for the direct election of the President and Vice President of the United States.
Sponsor: Rep. Cohen, Steve [D-TN-9] (Introduced 01/03/2019)
Cosponsors (11)

1337. H.J.RES.8
Proposing an amendment to the Constitution of the United States lim-

iting the pardon power of the President.
Sponsor: Rep. Cohen, Steve [D-TN-9] (Introduced 01/03/2019)
Cosponsors (16)

1338. H.J.RES.9
Proposing an amendment to the Constitution of the United States to protect the voting rights of the citizens of the United States.
Sponsor: Rep. Engel, Eliot L. [D-NY-16] (Introduced 01/03/2019)
Cosponsors (1)

1339. H.J.RES.10
Proposing an amendment to the Constitution of the United States to prohibit Members of Congress from receiving compensation during a fiscal year unless both Houses of Congress have agreed to a concurrent resolution on the budget for that fiscal year prior to the beginning of that fiscal year.
Sponsor: Rep. Fitzpatrick, Brian K. [R-PA-1] (Introduced 01/03/2019)
Cosponsors (1)

1340. H.J.RES.11
Proposing an amendment to the Constitution of the United States to provide for balanced budgets for the Government.
Sponsor: Rep. Fitzpatrick, Brian K. [R-PA-1] (Introduced 01/03/2019)
Cosponsors (1)

1341. H.J.RES.12
Proposing an amendment to the Constitution of the United States to limit the number of terms an individual may serve as a Member of Congress.
Sponsor: Rep. Fitzpatrick, Brian K. [R-PA-1] (Introduced 01/03/2019)
Cosponsors (3)

1342. H.J.RES.13
Proposing an amendment to the Constitution of the United States to clarify the presidential pardoning power.
Sponsor: Rep. Green, Al [D-TX-9] (Introduced 01/03/2019)
Cosponsors (0)

1343 H.J.RES.14
Proposing an amendment to the Constitution of the United States to limit the number of terms that a Member of Congress may serve to four

in the House of Representatives and two in the Senate.
Sponsor: Rep. Hollingsworth, Trey [R-IN-9] (Introduced 01/03/2019)
Cosponsors (1)

1344. H.J.RES.15
Proposing an amendment to the Constitution of the United States to end the practice of including more than one subject in a single law by requiring that each law enacted by Congress be limited to only one subject and that the subject be clearly and descriptively expressed in the title of the law.
Sponsor: Rep. Marino, Tom [R-PA-12] (Introduced 01/03/2019)
Cosponsors (0)

1345. H.J.RES.16
Proposing an amendment to the Constitution of the United States to limit the number of years an individual may serve as a Member of Congress.
Sponsor: Rep. Marino, Tom [R-PA-12] (Introduced 01/03/2019)
Cosponsors (1)

1346. H.J.RES.17
Proposing an amendment to the Constitution of the United States regarding health care.
Sponsor: Rep. McCollum, Betty [D-MN-4] (Introduced 01/03/2019)
Cosponsors (2)

1347. H.J.RES.18
Proposing an amendment to the Constitution of the United States to prohibit Members of Congress from receiving compensation for any period during which a Government shutdown is in effect.
Sponsor: Rep. Norman, Ralph [R-SC-5] (Introduced 01/03/2019)
Cosponsors (18)

1348 H.J.RES.19
Proposing an amendment to the Constitution of the United States to allow Congress to limit the number of terms that Representatives and Senators may serve.
Sponsor: Rep. Norman, Ralph [R-SC-5] (Introduced 01/03/2019)
Cosponsors (0)

1349. H.J.RES.20

Proposing an amendment to the Constitution of the United States to limit the number of terms that a Member of Congress may serve.

Sponsor: Rep. Rooney, Francis [R-FL-19] (Introduced 01/03/2019)

Cosponsors (56)

1350. H.J.RES.21

Proposing an amendment to the Constitution of the United States giving Congress power to regulate campaign contributions for Federal elections.

Sponsor: Rep. Schrader, Kurt [D-OR-5] (Introduced 01/03/2019)

Cosponsors (0)

1351. H.J.RES.22

Proposing a balanced budget amendment to the Constitution of the United States.

Sponsor: Rep. Chabot, Steve [R-OH-1] (Introduced 01/08/2019)

Cosponsors (41)

1352. H.J.RES.23

Proposing an amendment to the Constitution of the United States extending the right to vote to citizens sixteen years of age or older.

Sponsor: Rep. Meng, Grace [D-NY-6] (Introduced 01/09/2019)

Cosponsors (9)

1353. H.J.RES.24

Proposing an amendment to the Constitution of the United States regarding Presidential election voting rights for residents of all United States territories and commonwealths.

Sponsor: Del. Plaskett, Stacey E. [D-VI-At Large] (Introduced 01/09/2019)

Cosponsors (1)

1354. H.J.RES.25

Proposing an amendment to the Constitution of the United States to limit the number of terms a Representative or Senator may serve.

Sponsor: Rep. Byrne, Bradley [R-AL-1] (Introduced 01/10/2019)

Cosponsors (3)

1355. H.J.RES.26

Proposing an amendment to the Constitution of the United States to in-

crease the term of service of Members of the House of Representatives from 2 years to 4 years.
Sponsor: Rep. Marino, Tom [R-PA-12] (Introduced 01/11/2019)
Cosponsors (0)

1356. H.J.RES.29
Proposing an amendment to the Constitution of the United States to limit the number of terms an individual may serve as a Member of Congress.
Sponsor: Rep. Holding, George [R-NC-2] (Introduced 01/15/2019)
Cosponsors (3)

1357. H.J.RES.32
Proposing an amendment to the Constitution of the United States to give States the authority to repeal Federal rules and regulations when the repeal is agreed to by the legislatures of two-thirds of the several States.
Sponsor: Rep. Bishop, Rob [R-UT-1] (Introduced 01/22/2019)
Cosponsors (6)

1358. H.J.RES.33
Proposing an amendment to the Constitution of the United States relating to contributions and expenditures with respect to Federal elections.
Sponsor: Rep. Yarmuth, John A. [D-KY-3] (Introduced 01/24/2019)
Cosponsors (3)

1359. H.J.RES.34
Proposing an amendment to the Constitution of the United States to provide that Representatives shall be apportioned among the several States according to their respective numbers, counting the number of persons in each State who are citizens of the United States.
Sponsor: Rep. Davidson, Warren [R-OH-8] (Introduced 01/24/2019)
Cosponsors (11)

1360. H.J.RES.35
Proposing an amendment to the Constitution of the United States relative to equal rights for men and women.
Sponsor: Rep. Maloney, Carolyn B. [D-NY-12] (Introduced 01/29/2019)
Cosponsors (180)

1361. H.J.RES.36
Proposing an amendment to the Constitution of the United States relat-

ing to parental rights.
Sponsor: Rep. Banks, Jim [R-IN-3] (Introduced 01/30/2019)
Cosponsors (19)

***1362. H.J.RES.38**
Removing the deadline for the ratification of the equal rights amendment.
Sponsor: Rep. Speier, Jackie [D-CA-14] (Introduced 01/30/2019)
Cosponsors (218)

1363. H.J.RES.39
Proposing an amendment to the Constitution of the United States waiving the application of the first article of amendment to the political speech of corporations and other business organizations with respect to the disbursement of funds in connection with public elections and granting Congress and the States the power to establish limits on contributions and expenditures in elections for public office.
Sponsor: Rep. Kaptur, Marcy [D-OH-9] (Introduced 01/30/2019)
Cosponsors (1)

1364. H.J.RES.40
Proposing an amendment to the Constitution of the United States requiring that the Federal budget be balanced.
Sponsor: Rep. Loudermilk, Barry [R-GA-11] (Introduced 01/30/2019)
Cosponsors (10)

1365. H.J.RES.47
Proposing an amendment to the Constitution of the United States to repeal the sixteenth article of amendment.
Sponsor: Rep. King, Steve [R-IA-4] (Introduced 02/22/2019)
Cosponsors (1)

1366. H.J.RES.48
Proposing an amendment to the Constitution of the United States providing that the rights extended by the Constitution are the rights of natural persons only.
Sponsor: Rep. Jayapal, Pramila [D-WA-7] (Introduced 02/22/2019)
Cosponsors (74)

1367. H.J.RES.49
Proposing an amendment to the Constitution of the United States to

provide that Representatives shall be apportioned among the several States according to their respective numbers, counting the number of persons in each State who are citizens of the United States.
Sponsor: Rep. King, Steve [R-IA-4] (Introduced 02/25/2019)
Cosponsors (0)

1368. H.J.RES.50
Proposing a balanced budget amendment to the Constitution requiring that each agency and department's funding is justified.
Sponsor: Rep. Perry, Scott [R-PA-10] (Introduced 03/12/2019)
Cosponsors (2)

1369. H.J.RES.51
Proposing a balanced budget amendment to the Constitution of the United States.
Sponsor: Rep. Ratcliffe, John [R-TX-4] (Introduced 03/14/2019)
Cosponsors (5)

1370. H.J.RES.52
Proposing an amendment to the Constitution of the United States to require that the Supreme Court of the United States be composed of nine justices.
Sponsor: Rep. Green, Mark E. [R-TN-7] (Introduced 03/21/2019)
Cosponsors (5)

1371. H.J.RES.53
Proposing an amendment to the Constitution of the United States to require that the Supreme Court be composed of not more than nine justices.
Sponsor: Rep. Gallagher, Mike [R-WI-8] (Introduced 03/25/2019)
Cosponsors (21)

1372. H.J.RES.54: Proposing an amendment to the Constitution of the United States recognizing and securing the fundamental right to life, liberty, and property, which includes housing, health care, education, and nutrition.
Sponsor: Rep. Adams, Alma S. [D-NC-12] (Introduced 03/28/2019)
Cosponsors (3)

1373. H.J.RES.55
Proposing a balanced budget amendment to the Constitution of the

United States.
Sponsor: Rep. McAdams, Ben [D-UT-4] (Introduced 04/09/2019)
Cosponsors (12)

1374. H.J.RES.57
Proposing an amendment to the Constitution of the United States relating to the authority of Congress and the States to regulate contributions and expenditures in political campaigns and to enact public financing systems for such campaigns.
Sponsor: Rep. Schiff, Adam B. [D-CA-28] (Introduced 05/08/2019)
Cosponsors (16)

1375. H.J.RES.68
Proposing a balanced budget amendment to the Constitution of the United States.
Sponsor: Rep. Green, Mark E. [R-TN-7] (Introduced 06/20/2019)
Cosponsors (0)

1376. H.J.RES.69
Proposing an amendment to the Constitution of the United States to require the United States and the States to jointly ensure a high-quality education to all persons within the United States.
Sponsor: Rep. DeSaulnier, Mark [D-CA-11] (Introduced 06/26/2019)
Cosponsors (0)

1377. H.J.RES.70
Proposing an amendment to the Constitution of the United States prohibiting the delegation of the legislative powers granted to Congress.
Sponsor: Rep. Perry, Scott [R-PA-10] (Introduced 06/26/2019)
Cosponsors (0)

1378. H.J.RES.71
Proposing an amendment to the Constitution of the United States to require legislative approval for certain regulations.
Sponsor: Rep. Perry, Scott [R-PA-10] (Introduced 06/26/2019)
Cosponsors (0)

1379. H.J.RES.73
Proposing an amendment to the Constitution of the United States regarding the permissible sources of funding for elections for public office and State ballot measures.

Sponsor: Rep. McNerney, Jerry [D-CA-9] (Introduced 07/18/2019)
Cosponsors (2)

1380. H.J.RES.79

Removing the deadline for the ratification of the equal rights amendment.
Sponsor: Rep. Speier, Jackie [D-CA-14] (Introduced 11/08/2019)
Cosponsors (224)

1381. H.J.RES.86

Proposing an amendment to the Constitution of the United States to limit the number of consecutive terms that a Member of Congress may serve.
Sponsor: Rep. Timmons, William R. IV [R-SC-4] (Introduced 03/05/2020)
Cosponsors (1)

1382. H.J.RES.91

Proposing an amendment to the Constitution of the United States protecting the right of citizens to vote.
Sponsor: Rep. Cooper, Jim [D-TN-5] (Introduced 06/25/2020)
Cosponsors (0)

1383. H.J.RES.92

Proposing an amendment to the Constitution of the United States to prohibit the use of slavery and involuntary servitude as a punishment for a crime.
Sponsor: Rep. Richmond, Cedric L. [D-LA-2] (Introduced 06/29/2020)
Cosponsors (4)

1384. H.J.RES.93

Proposing an amendment to the Constitution of the United States regarding the right to vote.
Sponsor: Rep. Pocan, Mark [D-WI-2] (Introduced 08/07/2020)
Cosponsors (41)

1385. H.J.RES.95

Proposing an amendment to the Constitution of the United States to require that the Supreme Court of the United States be composed of nine justices.
Sponsor: Rep. Peterson, Collin C. [D-MN-7] (Introduced 09/24/2020)
Cosponsors (5)

1386. H.J.RES.96

Proposing an amendment to the Constitution of the United States to ensure that an Act of Congress that increases the number of judges comprising the Supreme Court may not take effect before the date that is 10 years after the date of the enactment of such Act.

Sponsor: Rep. Collins, Doug [R-GA-9] (Introduced 09/29/2020)

Cosponsors (11)

1387. H.J.RES.97

Proposing an amendment to the Constitution of the United States to limit the composition of the Senate to Senators from States admitted to the Union prior to the One Hundred Sixteenth Congress.

Sponsor: Rep. Walker, Mark [R-NC-6] (Introduced 09/29/2020)

Cosponsors (0)

1388. H.J.RES.98

Proposing an amendment to the Constitution of the United States to repeal the twenty-third article of amendment to the Constitution of the United States.

Sponsor: Rep. Johnson, Dusty [R-SD-At Large] (Introduced 10/06/2020)

Cosponsors (0)

1389. H.J.RES.99

Proposing a balanced budget amendment to the Constitution of the United States.

Sponsor: Rep. Amash, Justin [L-MI-3] (Introduced 10/09/2020)

Cosponsors (0)

1390. H.J.RES.104

Proposing an amendment to the Constitution of the United States to prohibit the use of slavery and involuntary servitude as a punishment for a crime.

Sponsor: Rep. Clay, Wm. Lacy [D-MO-1] (Introduced 12/02/2020)

Cosponsors (20)

1391. H.J.RES.106

Proposing an amendment to the Constitution of the United States to prohibit the use of slavery and involuntary servitude as a punishment for a crime.

Sponsor: Rep. Hall, Kwanza [D-GA-5] (Introduced 12/16/2020)

Cosponsors (0)

1392. H.J.RES.108
Proposing a balanced budget amendment to the Constitution of the United States.
Sponsor: Rep. Amash, Justin [L-MI-3] (Introduced 12/18/2020)
Cosponsors (0)

1393. H.J.RES.109
Proposing an amendment to the Constitution of the United States [providing for equality before the law].
Sponsor: Rep. Amash, Justin [L-MI-3] (Introduced 12/18/2020)
Cosponsors (0)

Senate

1394. S.J.RES.1
A joint resolution proposing an amendment to the Constitution of the United States relative to limiting the number of terms that a Member of Congress may serve.
Sponsor: Sen. Cruz, Ted [R-TX] (Introduced 01/03/2019)
Cosponsors (15)

1395. S.J.RES.3
A joint resolution proposing an amendment to the Constitution of the United States relative to balancing the budget.
Sponsor: Sen. Hyde-Smith, Cindy [R-MS] (Introduced 01/04/2019)
Cosponsors (23)

1396. S.J.RES.5
A joint resolution proposing an amendment to the Constitution of the United States requiring that the Federal budget be balanced.
Sponsor: Sen. Lee, Mike [R-UT] (Introduced 01/24/2019)
Cosponsors (1)

***1397. S.J.RES.6**
A joint resolution removing the deadline for the ratification of the equal rights amendment.
Sponsor: Sen. Cardin, Benjamin L. [D-MD] (Introduced 01/25/2019)
Cosponsors (48)

1398. S.J.RES.14
A joint resolution proposing an amendment to the Constitution of the United States to require that the Supreme Court of the United States be composed of not more than 9 justices.
Sponsor: Sen. Rubio, Marco [R-FL] (Introduced 03/25/2019)
Cosponsors (22)

1399. S.J.RES.15
A joint resolution proposing an amendment to the Constitution of the United States relative to equal rights for men and women.
Sponsor: Sen. Menendez, Robert [D-NJ] (Introduced 03/27/2019)
Cosponsors (23)

1400. S.J.RES.16
A joint resolution proposing an amendment to the Constitution of the United States to abolish the electoral college and to provide for the direct election of the President and Vice President of the United States.
Sponsor: Sen. Merkley, Jeff [D-OR] (Introduced 03/28/2019)
Cosponsors (2)

1401. S.J.RES.17
A joint resolution proposing an amendment to the Constitution of the United States to abolish the electoral college and to provide for the direct election of the President and Vice President of the United States.
Sponsor: Sen. Schatz, Brian [D-HI] (Introduced 04/02/2019)
Cosponsors (3)

1402. S.J.RES.18
A joint resolution proposing a balanced budget amendment to the Constitution of the United States.
Sponsor: Sen. Tester, Jon [D-MT] (Introduced 04/04/2019)
Cosponsors (2)

1403. S.J.RES.19
A joint resolution proposing an amendment to the Constitution of the United States to require (except during time of war and subject to suspension by Congress) that the total amount of money expended by the United States during any fiscal year not exceed the amount of certain revenue received by the United States during such fiscal year and not exceed 20 percent of the gross domestic product of the United States during the previous calendar year.
Sponsor: Sen. Shelby, Richard C. [R-AL] (Introduced 05/02/2019)
Cosponsors (0)

1404. S.J.RES.21
A joint resolution proposing amendments to the Constitution of the United States relative to the line item veto, a limitation on the number of terms that a Member of Congress may serve, and requiring a vote of two-thirds of the membership of both Houses of Congress on any legislation raising or imposing new taxes or fees.
Sponsor: Sen. Scott, Rick [R-FL] (Introduced 05/14/2019)
Cosponsors (0)

1405. S.J.RES.49
A joint resolution proposing an amendment to the Constitution of the United States authorizing the Congress to prohibit the physical desecration of the flag of the United States.
Sponsor: Sen. Daines, Steve [R-MT] (Introduced 06/13/2019)
Cosponsors (9)

1406. S.J.RES.51
A joint resolution proposing an amendment to the Constitution of the United States relating to contributions and expenditures intended to affect elections.
Sponsor: Sen. Udall, Tom [D-NM] (Introduced 07/30/2019)
Cosponsors (46)

1407. S.J.RES.70
A joint resolution proposing an amendment to the Constitution of the United States relative to the voting threshold for impeachment.
Sponsor: Sen. Scott, Rick [R-FL] (Introduced 02/13/2020)
Cosponsors (0)

1408. S.J.RES.75
A joint resolution proposing an amendment to the Constitution of the United States relative to the fundamental right to vote.
Sponsor: Sen. Durbin, Richard J. [D-IL] (Introduced 08/04/2020)
Cosponsors (8)

1409. S.J.RES.76
A joint resolution proposing an amendment to the Constitution of the United States to require that the Supreme Court of the United States be composed of nine justices.
Sponsor: Sen. Cruz, Ted [R-TX] (Introduced 10/19/2020)
Cosponsors (15)

1410. S.J.RES.81 A joint resolution proposing an amendment to the Constitution of the United States to prohibit the use of slavery and involuntary servitude as a punishment for a crime.
Sponsor: Sen. Merkley, Jeff [D-OR] (Introduced 12/02/2020)
Cosponsors (4)

117th Congress (2021-2022)

House

1411. H.J.RES.1
Proposing an amendment to the Constitution of the United States relating to contributions and expenditures intended to affect elections.
Sponsor: Rep. Deutch, Theodore E. [D-FL-22] (Introduced 01/04/2021)
Cosponsors (75)

1412. H.J.RES.2
Proposing an amendment to the Constitution of the United States relative to balancing the budget.
Sponsor: Rep. Buchanan, Vern [R-FL-16] (Introduced 01/04/2021)
Cosponsors (0)

1413. H.J.RES.3
Proposing a balanced budget amendment to the Constitution of the United States.
Sponsor: Rep. Chabot, Steve [R-OH-1] (Introduced 01/04/2021)
Cosponsors (40)

1414. H.J.RES.4
Proposing an amendment to the Constitution of the United States limiting the pardon power of the President.
Sponsor: Rep. Cohen, Steve [D-TN-9] (Introduced 01/04/2021)
Cosponsors (15)

1415. H.J.RES.5
Proposing an amendment to the Constitution of the United States protecting the right of citizens to vote.
Sponsor: Rep. Cooper, Jim [D-TN-5] (Introduced 01/04/2021)
Cosponsors (0)

1416. H.J.RES.6: Proposing an amendment to the Constitution of the United States to limit the number of terms an individual may serve as a Member of Congress.

Sponsor: Rep. Fitzpatrick, Brian K. [R-PA-1] (Introduced 01/04/2021)
Cosponsors (3)

1417. H.J.RES.7
Proposing an amendment to the Constitution of the United States to prohibit Members of Congress from receiving compensation during a fiscal year unless both Houses of Congress have agreed to a concurrent resolution on the budget for that fiscal year prior to the beginning of that fiscal year.
Sponsor: Rep. Fitzpatrick, Brian K. [R-PA-1] (Introduced 01/04/2021)
Cosponsors (2)

1418. H.J.RES.8
Proposing an amendment to the Constitution of the United States to provide for balanced budgets for the Government.
Sponsor: Rep. Fitzpatrick, Brian K. [R-PA-1] (Introduced 01/04/2021)
Cosponsors (1)

1419. H.J.RES.9
Proposing an amendment to the Constitution of the United States to limit the number of terms that a Member of Congress may serve to four in the House of Representatives and two in the Senate.
Sponsor: Rep. Hollingsworth, Trey [R-IN-9] (Introduced 01/04/2021)
Cosponsors (0)

1420. H.J.RES.11
Proposing an amendment to the Constitution of the United States to require that the Supreme Court of the United States be composed of nine justices.
Sponsor: Rep. Johnson, Dusty [R-SD-At Large] (Introduced 01/04/2021)
Cosponsors (173)

1421. H.J.RES.12
Proposing an amendment to the Constitution of the United States to limit the number of terms that a Member of Congress may serve.
Sponsor: Rep. Norman, Ralph [R-SC-5] (Introduced 01/04/2021)
Cosponsors (65)

1422. H.J.RES.13: Proposing a balanced budget amendment to the Constitution requiring that each agency and department's funding is justified.

Sponsor: Rep. Perry, Scott [R-PA-10] (Introduced 01/04/2021)
Cosponsors (2)

1423 H.J.RES.14
Proposing an amendment to the Constitution of the United States to abolish the electoral college and to provide for the direct election of the President and Vice President of the United States.
Sponsor: Rep. Cohen, Steve [D-TN-9] (Introduced 01/11/2021)
Cosponsors (8)

***1424. H.J.RES.17**
Removing the deadline for the ratification of the equal rights amendment.
Sponsor: Rep. Speier, Jackie [D-CA-14] (Introduced 01/21/2021)
Cosponsors (214)

1425. H.J.RES.18
Proposing an amendment to the Constitution of the United States to limit the number of terms that a Member of Congress may serve.
Sponsor: Rep. Hern, Kevin [R-OK-1] (Introduced 01/25/2021)
Cosponsors (0)

1426. H.J.RES.19
Proposing an amendment to the Constitution of the United States to repeal the twenty-third article of amendment to the Constitution of the United States.
Sponsor: Rep. Johnson, Dusty [R-SD-At Large] (Introduced 01/25/2021)
Cosponsors (14)

1427. H.J.RES.20
Proposing an amendment to the Constitution of the United States recognizing and securing the fundamental right to life, liberty, and property, which includes housing, health care, education, and nutrition.
Sponsor: Rep. Adams, Alma S. [D-NC-12] (Introduced 01/28/2021)
Cosponsors (2)

1428. H.J.RES.21
Proposing an amendment to the Constitution of the United States giving Congress power to regulate campaign contributions for Federal elections.
Sponsor: Rep. Schrader, Kurt [D-OR-5] (Introduced 01/28/2021)
Cosponsors (0)

1429. H.J.RES.23

Proposing an amendment to the Constitution of the United States extending the right to vote to citizens sixteen years of age or older.

Sponsor: Rep. Meng, Grace [D-NY-6] (Introduced 02/03/2021)

Cosponsors (17)

1430. H.J.RES.24

Proposing an amendment to the Constitution of the United States to provide that Representatives shall be apportioned among the several States according to their respective numbers, counting the number of persons in each State who are citizens of the United States.

Sponsor: Rep. Davidson, Warren [R-OH-8] (Introduced 02/04/2021)

Cosponsors (15)

1431. H.J.RES.26

Proposing an amendment to the Constitution of the United States requiring that the Federal budget be balanced.

Sponsor: Rep. Loudermilk, Barry [R-GA-11] (Introduced 02/18/2021)

Cosponsors (6)

1432. H.J.RES.28

Proposing an amendment to the Constitution of the United States relative to equal rights for men and women.

Sponsor: Rep. Maloney, Carolyn B. [D-NY-12] (Introduced 02/26/2021)

Cosponsors (98)

1433. H.J.RES.30

Proposing a balanced budget amendment to the Constitution of the United States.

Sponsor: Rep. Green, Mark E. [R-TN-7] (Introduced 03/09/2021)

Cosponsors (0)

1434. H.J.RES.31

Proposing an amendment to the Constitution of the United States relative to equal rights for men and women.

Sponsor: Rep. Smith, Christopher H. [R-NJ-4] (Introduced 03/16/2021)

Cosponsors (0)

1435. H.J.RES.32

Proposing a balanced budget amendment to the Constitution of the United States.

Sponsor: Rep. Obernolte, Jay [R-CA-8] (Introduced 03/19/2021)
Cosponsors (0)

1436. H.J.RES.39
Proposing an amendment to the Constitution of the United States to require that the Supreme Court be composed of not more than nine justices.
Sponsor: Rep. Gallagher, Mike [R-WI-8] (Introduced 04/13/2021)
Cosponsors (8)

1437. H.J.RES.40: Proposing an amendment to the Constitution of the United States to require that the Supreme Court of the United States be composed of nine justices.
Sponsor: Rep. Biggs, Andy [R-AZ-5] (Introduced 04/15/2021)
Cosponsors (12)

1438. H.J.RES.42 :Proposing an amendment to the Constitution of the United States to provide that a new State may only be admitted into the Union upon a vote of two-thirds of each House of Congress.
Sponsor: Rep. McClintock, Tom [R-CA-4] (Introduced 04/21/2021)
Cosponsors (4)

1439. H.J.RES.43
Proposing an amendment to the Constitution of the United States to require that the Supreme Court of the United States be composed of nine justices.
Sponsor: Rep. Green, Mark E. [R-TN-7] (Introduced 04/22/2021)
Cosponsors (0)

1440. H.J.RES.44
Proposing an amendment to the Constitution of the United States regarding health care.
Sponsor: Rep. McCollum, Betty [D-MN-4] (Introduced 04/22/2021)
Cosponsors (3)

1441. H.J.RES.45
Proposing an amendment to the Constitution of the United States to clarify the presidential pardoning power.
Sponsor: Rep. Green, Al [D-TX-9] (Introduced 04/22/2021)
Cosponsors (0)

1442. H.J.RES.47

Proposing an amendment to the Constitution of the United States to require three-fifths majorities for bills increasing taxes.
Sponsor: Rep. Green, Mark E. [R-TN-7] (Introduced 05/20/2021)
Cosponsors (0)

1443. H.J.RES.48

Proposing an amendment to the Constitution of the United States providing that the rights extended by the Constitution are the rights of natural persons only.
Sponsor: Rep. Jayapal, Pramila [D-WA-7] (Introduced 05/20/2021)
Cosponsors (57)

Senate

***1444. S.J.RES.1**
A joint resolution removing the deadline for the ratification of the equal rights amendment.
Sponsor: Sen. Cardin, Benjamin L. [D-MD] (Introduced 01/22/2021)
Cosponsors (4)

1445. S.J.RES.2
A joint resolution proposing amendments to the Constitution of the United States relative to the line item veto, a limitation on the number of terms that a Member of Congress may serve, and requiring a vote of two-thirds of the membership of both Houses of Congress on any legislation raising or imposing new taxes or fees.
Sponsor: Sen. Scott, Rick [R-FL] (Introduced 01/22/2021)
Cosponsors (0)

1446. S.J.RES.3
A joint resolution proposing an amendment to the Constitution of the United States relative to limiting the number of terms that a Member of Congress may serve.
Sponsor: Sen. Cruz, Ted [R-TX] (Introduced 01/22/2021)
Cosponsors (14)

1447. S.J.RES.4
A joint resolution proposing an amendment to the Constitution of the United States to require that the Supreme Court of the United States be composed of not more than 9 justices.
Sponsor: Sen. Rubio, Marco [R-FL] (Introduced 01/22/2021)
Cosponsors (17)

1448. S.J.RES.5
A joint resolution proposing an amendment to the Constitution of the United States requiring that the Federal budget be balanced.
Sponsor: Sen. Lee, Mike [R-UT] (Introduced 01/22/2021)
Cosponsors (1)

1449. S.J.RES.6
A joint resolution proposing an amendment to the Constitution of the United States relative to balancing the budget.
Sponsor: Sen. Hyde-Smith, Cindy [R-MS] (Introduced 02/03/2021)
Cosponsors (15)

1450.. S.J.RES.9
A joint resolution proposing an amendment to the Constitution of the United States to require that the Supreme Court of the United States be composed of nine justices.
Sponsor: Sen. Cruz, Ted [R-TX] (Introduced 02/25/2021)
Cosponsors (19)

1451. S.J.RES.11
A joint resolution proposing an amendment to the Constitution of the United States to clarify the authority of Congress and the States to regulate corporations, limited liability companies, and other corporate entities established by the laws of any State, the United States, or any foreign state.
Sponsor: Sen. Tester, Jon [D-MT] (Introduced 03/15/2021)
Cosponsors (0)

1452. S.J.RES.12
A joint resolution proposing an amendment to the Constitution of the United States which requires (except during time of war and subject to suspension by Congress) that the total amount of money expended by the United States during any fiscal year not exceed the amount of certain revenue received by the United States during such fiscal year and not exceed 20 percent of the gross domestic product of the United States during the previous calendar year.
Sponsor: Sen. Shelby, Richard C. [R-AL] (Introduced 03/18/2021)
Cosponsors (0)

1453. S.J.RES.18. A joint resolution proposing an amendment to the Constitution of the United States to repeal the twenty-third article of amendment to the Constitution of the United States. Sponsor **Sen. Marshall Roger W. (R-KS) (**Introduced 04/22/2021**) Cosponsors (0)**

SUBJECT INDEX for 2001-2022 (second part of 102nd – first part of 117th Congress)

(Note: The numbers in this index refer to the numbers at the beginning of each entry. These begin, where the last volume left off, at number 692.)

SPONSOR INDEX

(Note: The numbers in this index refer to the numbers at the beginning of each entry. These begin, where Vol. 3 left off, at number 692. Members of the House will have a district number after their states' designations; Senators will not.)

About the Author

Dr. John R. Vile (Ph.D., University of Virginia) is a Professor of Political Science and Dean of the University Honors College at Middle Tennessee State University. He has written the *Encyclopedia of Constitutional Amendments, Proposed Amendments, and Amending Issues: 1789-2015*, now in its fourth edition, as well as several other books on the amending process including *Conventional Wisdom: The Alternate Article V Mechanism for Proposing Amendments to the U.S. Constitution* (2016), *The Constitutional Amending Process in American Political Thought, Constitutional Change in the United States*, and *Contemporary Questions Surrounding the Constitutional Amending Process.* He is the author of *The Constitutional Convention of 1787: A Comprehensive Encyclopedia of America's Founding*, which is now in a revised edition, as well as *A Companion to the U.S. Constitution and Its Amendments* (7th ed., 2021) and *Essential Supreme Court Decisions: Summaries of Leading Cases in U.S. Constitutional Law* (18th ed., 2022). Other recent books include *America's National Anthem: "The Star-Spangled Banner" in U.S. History, Culture and Law* (2021); *The Bible in American Law and Politics: A Reference Guide* (2020); *The Liberty Bell and Its Legacy: An Encyclopedia of an American Icon in U.S. History and Culture* (2020); *The Declaration of Independence: America's First Founding Document in U.S. History and Culture* (2019); *More Than a Plea for a Declaration of Rights: The Constitutional and Political Thought of Georgia Mason of Virginia* (2019); *A Constellation of Great Men: Exploring the Character Sketches of Dr. Benjamin Rush of Pennsylvania of the Signers of the Declaration of Independence* (2019); *The American Flag: An Encyclopedia of the Stars and Stripes in U.S. History, Culture and Law* (2018), *Governmental Responses to Natural Disasters in the U.S.: A Documentary History* (2018); *The Wisest Council in the World: Restoring the Character Sketches by William Pierce of Georgia of the Delegates to the Constitutional Convention of 1787* (2015); *Re-Framers: 170 Eccentric, Visionary, and Patriotic Proposals to Rewrite the U.S. Constitution* (2014); *The Men Who Made The Constitution: Lives of the Delegates to the Constitutional Convention* (2013); *The Writing and Ratification of the U.S. Constitution: Practical Virtue In Action* (2012), and others. He is a coauthor of *Constitutional Law in Contemporary America* and one of the original editors of and contributors to *The Encyclopedia of the First Amendment* and *The Encyclopedia of the Fourth Amendment*, and he continues contributing to the on-line version of the former, which is at https://mtsu.edu/first-amendment/encyclopedia/ Vile is the editor of *Great American Lawyers: An Encyclopedia* (2001); and *Great American Judges: An Encyclopedia* (2003), and he has written introductions for a number of historical reprints by the Lawbook Exchange. Vile has been designated as the Phi Kappa Phi Scholar for 2020-2022.

www.ingramcontent.com/pod-product-compliance
Lightning Source LLC
LaVergne TN
LVHW062125200926
848484LV00007B/1766
* 9 7 8 1 6 1 6 1 9 6 5 7 8 *